William Still

Talks To The Children

D1492944

Christian Focus Publications Ltd.

Published By
Christian Focus Publications Ltd
Geanies House, Fearn IV20 1TW
Ross-shire, Scotland, UK

ISBN 0 906731 992

Contents

Page

Mr. Still has introduced each section with an appropiate sentence that summarises the suitability of teaching these subjects to children.

In some of the addresses, Mr. Still engages in dialogue with his young hearers.

Foreword To Children's Addresses

These children's addresses have been gathered by Aileen Stewart from over nine hundred given on Sunday mornings in Gilcomston South Church. Most of them were given to little ones aged between three and seven years, although during the summer when Primary Sunday School was suspended, opportunity was taken to speak to a somewhat older age group, say from seven to ten years.

The intention of the addresses is to teach little ones the same basic lesson from the Word, as far as possible, as is given to the grown-ups; and to instruct them in sound biblical doctrine from the earliest years of their understanding. Experience has shown that little ones brought up and nurtured in truly Christian homes - and even those who are not but are roped into Sunday School, prove to have remarkable understanding of spiritual things and can become quite hungry for knowledge of the Bible and the Gospel.

Miss Stewart has sought to arrange the addresses under appropriate subject headings.

William Still
20th April, 1989

7

Introductory Chapter On Teaching
Children   Theology

Although the practice of addressing children, particularly at morning services on the Lord's Day, is almost universal in the Church of Scotland, years of the present ministry elapsed before it was attempted. I had, of course, for perhaps twelve years led the children's work on Sunday afternoons in a children's church, and on relinquishing that, felt that I ought still to play a specific part in the education of the little ones, although fully trusting those subsequently appointed to the task. Hence the commencement of children's addresses during morning worship.

I had long deplored that children's addresses in worship were so often means of diversion and entertainment (not only to children) rather than means of biblical education. It was therefore my determination to teach the little ones sound biblical doctrine, however simply and attractively it had to be done.

Perhaps it was natural, then, that since after eighteen months of topical preaching from individual texts, the hunger of the people for the Word of God was such that systematic biblical exposition was called for and embarked upon in normal worship (taking a book of the Bible, Old Testament and New alternately morning and evening) it seemed logical to seek to relate what was said to the children in the sermon.

This has been a most taxing endeavour; for often, the portion of Scripture appointed to be dealt with was such as did not seem to promise clear and attractive presentation to children. But since no time was wasted determining the theme of the sermon and preparation was begun early in the week, there was ample time for thought and prayer to decide how to gear the Word to children.

That it was pleasing to God that this should be done was made plain by the fact that although frequently near the end of the week before light came, it always did, and the Word to the children was made to bear some relation to that spoken to the grown-ups. The main point might not always be the same in both, but it was always germane to the passage of Scripture read, the earnest intent being that ethics should always be related to faith and doctrine.

Underlying the desire to teach little children sound biblical doctrine there is the biblical doctrine and practice of infant baptism. A full understanding of the covenant of grace is therefore essential to the bringing up of children in the Lord. In seeking to teach little children from earliest understanding the truths of their covenant baptism (which may be earlier than parents are prone to believe), one is astonished how beautifully their dawning intelligence responds. Answers to questions asked may be so penetrating and telescopic that the lesson may be prematurely summed up by one devastating observation: "Out of the mouths of babes and sucklings!"

When little ones taught of the Lord in His Word understand so much of the saving and sanctifying truths of the Gospel, is it not a shame and a crying scandal, that they should be deprived of that Word which they may sometimes grasp more tellingly than their elders? Why should they be served a diet of trivialities, when there is all the glory of the Gospel for them to understand and learn to live by?

Why ministers, who are mostly parents themselves and presumably teach their own children the truths of the faith from earliest years, do not seek to do the same for the lambs under their shepherd care is a mystery. Could it be that an element of the theatrical, which can be innate in those called to public ministry, constitutes a real temptation merely to entertain? Having learned from experience something of the wisdom God imparts to little children, I regard it as an exceedingly solemn charge to treat them as one's most precious responsibility; and if what I have sought to do in these examples of children's addresses, culled from hundreds, encourages to that end, I will thank God.

Section One

Teaching Children About The Gospel

How rich and rare the Gospel is! Who should delight in it more than children, who have not lost their sense of wonder?

(1) Knowing God

(a) How do we know there is a God?
(Acts 28:26-27)

If some little boy or girl at Nursery School, who didn't believe in God at all, said to you, "How do you know that there is a God?" - what would you say? You can't see Him, can you? Although we have been speaking to Him here this morning, He is invisible. I used that word in prayer: He is "invisible" - you can't see Him with your eyes. So we don't need to close our eyes to speak to Him. But He is there all the same.

How would you try to show people that there is a God? Well, there are four ways that you can show them.

1. Who made the world?

"God."

Of course. He made the world with all its beauty. If some little one should say, maybe taught by a naughty Mummy or Daddy that the world made itself, you just laugh, Ha! Ha! Ha! The world made itself - what nonsense!

2. The second thing is this: God has given us a book. You know what it is called - the Bible. It tells us all about God from the beginning when He began to make the world.

3. Then, God has put something inside us - our conscience, that tells us (and every boy or girl has this, whether they know about Jesus or not) right and wrong. We know when we do wrong and we know when we do right. God put that in us.

4. Then, there is Jesus. He is not here now,

except by the Spirit. He is up in heaven with a wonderful body that will never wear out - an ever-lasting body. But He did come to earth about two thousand years ago. People wrote about Him and recorded what He said, and we know that Jesus did not tell lies. He not only tells us about God but He came from God. He came to save us from our sins and to give us His Holy Spirit into our hearts to help us in our conscience, not only to know what is right but to do what is right. It is one thing to know what is right but it is another thing to do it. We are not able to do it as we ought because we are poor, sinful, little monkeys. But when Jesus' Holy Spirit comes into our hearts He helps us and strengthens us to do what we know to be right and to refuse to do what we know to be wrong.

Will you think about that ? God shows Himself in what He has made, shows Himself in the Book He has given us, shows Himself in our conscience, and shows Himself perfectly and beautifully and wonderfully in Jesus our Saviour.

The golden sunshine, vernal air,
Sweet flowers and fruits Thy love declare
Where harvests ripen, Thou art there,
Who givest all.
Thou didst not spare Thine only Son
But gav'st Him for a world undone,
And freely with that blessed One
Thou givest all.

(b)Knowing God
(2 Timothy 1)

The Bible says that no one has ever seen God. Men have seen Jesus, God's Son, but never God the Father. This morning we closed our eyes for prayers and I spoke to Him. You, I am sure were following what I was saying and praying along with me. How do we know that there is a God the Father when no one has ever seen Him?

"Because He made the world."

That's right: He made the world. The writer to the Hebrews says, "God, who is invisible (you can't see Him with your eyes) made the things that are visible (the things we can see and touch)." And that is exactly what you said, my dear. That is right: God made the world. We have to believe that. But everybody doesn't believe it.

Let me ask you this: When did you see the wind? Have you ever seen the wind? You see what it does. It blows down trees - lots of them. But you don't see the wind. Then there are microbes which can make people sick. Doctors can only see them by looking through microscopes. They are so tiny you can't see them with your eyes. But they are there and make people ill. When do we see the waves that bring the sound of the radio to us, and the sound and colour of television? We don't see that. We don't see these things but we believe, because we see the result. We see the pictures on television; we hear the sound on the radio; we know that people are ill when the doctor says, "Oh yes, there's tiny germs there to be got rid of." So we believe that God is, that He is good, that He cares for us, and watches over us because we see His hand in nature.

But of course we believe also because Jesus tells us about His Father, and Jesus would not tell us any lies, would He? Oh no! Again, we believe there is a God because we know He is in our hearts. We take Him into our hearts, into our lives. We believe the Lord Jesus is there. Big folk do that and so do little folk whose Mummies and Daddies are Christians. Their parents say, "O Lord, come into my little boy's heart," or, "Come into my little girl's heart," (and they teach their children to pray that prayer for themselves) and they are sure that He does. They are certain because the Bible says that this is what happens.

When He is there, what happens? We learn to love Jesus. That is the proof that we know there is a God because when we take Jesus into our heart He teaches us to love Him and to love His Father and to love one another. It is all very wonderful, that God whom no one has ever seen, who made all the wonderful things there are in the world and came to tell us about Himself through His Son who died for us, can live in our hearts. He does this by placing His Spirit in our hearts.

> I see Thee not, I hear Thee not,
> Yet art Thou oft with me;
> And earth hath ne'er so dear a spot
> As where I meet with Thee.

> Yet, though I have not seen, and still
> Must rest in faith alone
> I love Thee, dearest Lord, and will,
> Unseen but not unknown.

(2) The Gospel

(a) God's Plan of Salvation
(1 Peter 3:18)

Today's message is not easy to understand. When God's bright angel who was called Lucifer (that is somebody who holds a light - a light bearer) spoiled God's beautiful, perfect world, God said to His Son, "What are We going to do? He has spoilt all Our beautiful world."

So They spoke together, the Father and the Son. They said, "We can't do anything with angels because when angels go bad they can't be changed. Therefore they cannot go to heaven because they are bad. We can't do anything with them. What are We going to do with the world? Can We change the trees, the stones, the rivers and the animals, for the whole world is ruined?"

The Son said, "I don't think so, for the animals and the trees don't understand."

"But," said the Father, "what about man?"

"Oh well," said the Son, "he is to blame because he agreed with Lucifer (who of course changed his name to Satan, the devil) and disobeyed Us. Is there anything We can do about man?"

The Father said, "That is very, very difficult. It is very difficult to change him because he has a mind. The animals don't have minds like him. There is only one way to change him, and that is from the inside. You, My Son, must go down to earth and change man from the inside."

"Oh!" said the Son who was always obedient to His Father even when it was hard. "All right, if that is the way to do it, I will go down to earth and change man from the inside. But how am I going to do it?"

"You will go down to earth; You will be born in Bethlehem as a baby of Mary; then You will grow up as a boy, and a bigger boy and a man. You will heal people, do wonderful miracles, teach people about My Word and then You will take all the badness of man into Your own body."

"Oh," said the Son, "that will be very sore (because there was no badness in Him. He was perfect.)"

"Yes," said the Father," You will have to take all the badness in man into Your body and *die with it*, and so destroy it and its power."

And that is what happened. Down came God's Son at Christmas time and was born as a baby in the stable in Bethlehem. He grew up and took all *our* sin upon Him and died with it to destroy it. And because His soul could not die He rose again on the third day. This is what Peter is telling us, as I read to you, "the righteous died for the unrighteous" (those who had sinned) to take away their sins. That's wonderful, isn't it? That is why Jesus came to earth to be born as a baby, and grew to be a man: so that He could take all our badness into His body, die with it and so destroy it. It is why we are so happy at Christmas time, as at other times, because Jesus came to take away all badness and to bring us to God.

(b) He died that we might be forgiven
(Luke 23:32-56)

In the first part of our reading this morning three sets of people said to Jesus when He was hanging on the Cross, "Why don't you save yourself if you are God's Son and can do everything, all sorts of miracles." We know that He did perform all kinds of wonderful miracles: healing people, giving them sight, even raising them from the dead. Three sets of people said to Jesus, "If you can do those wonderful miracles because you are the Son of God, why don't you save yourself?"

The rulers said it first, the people who had hung Him there. The Roman soldiers had nailed Him to the cross but it was at the command of the rulers, the Jewish leaders and Pilate. The soldiers said to Him, and they were jeering at Him, "Why don't you come down and save yourself? You say you are the Saviour. Come down and save yourself, if you can do miracles." The rulers said it, the soldiers said it, and then, one of the thieves said it. Remember there were three men crucified: a bad man at one side and a bad man at the other side and Jesus in the middle. Wasn't it awful to take Him and hang Him there with these two bad men? One of them said the same thing, "Why don't you save yourself and us?" I don't know if he was caring much about saving Jesus but he wanted his own life to be saved. He wanted to be taken off his cross. "Why can't you save yourself and us?"

Now, I want to ask you a question: Why didn't He? Well, if He had come down from the Cross and not died, our sins wouldn't have been taken away. He was there to bleed and die to take away our sins. But how was it that being nailed to that Cross and dying, He was able to take away our sins? If you know - and I think some of you do - you know something very, very important. It is very serious and grim and almost frightening, but it is true.

This morning we are going to find out how it was that Jesus hanging there on the Cross could take away our sins. What has killing people to do with sins? Why do we put people who steal into prison? We do it to punish them for their crimes. Jesus was being punished for our sins so that we would not be punished. Never, never, never forget it. Jesus is able to take away our sins because He paid the penalty for our sins. He took the punishment. Jesus hung on the cross and was punished to death for all our sins so that we could go free and not go to hell and away from God. That is the meaning of it.

Some people say that Jesus in the New Testament is much more forgiving than God is in the Old Testament. It is not true. If Jesus is so very forgiving - and of course He is- it is because He has paid our penalty. Jesus is forgiving. We heard what He said before He died to the people that were nailing Him to the cross: "Father, forgive them because they don't really know what they are doing." But this is how He is able to forgive so readily and gladly. It is not for nothing, it is not just because He feels nice towards us, it is not only because He is kind and loves us that He is able to forgive us. He has borne the punishment for our sins and is able, and willing, and glad to forgive us our sins just for that reason. He paid the price of all our naughtiness, and all our badness. If anyone asks you, "How was it that Jesus hanging on the Cross could forgive our sins?" say ,"It is because He bore the punishment for us." Never forget. This hymn will remind you.

> There is a green hill far away,
>   Without a city wall,
> Where the dear Lord was crucified,
>   Who died to save us all.
>
> We may not know, we cannot tell
>   What pains He had to bear;
> But we believe it was for us
>   He hung and suffered there.
>
> He died that we might be forgiven,
>   He died to make us good,
> That we might go at last to heaven,
>   Saved by His precious blood.
>
> There was no other good enough
>   To pay the price of sin;
> He only could unlock the gate
>   Of heaven and let us in.
>
> O dearly, dearly has He loved,
>   And we must love Him too,
> And trust in His redeeming blood,
>   And try His works to do.

(c)Jesus paid it all
(Colossians 2: 9-15)

When people go shopping, of course they have to pay for the things they buy. They have to take with them coins, or paper notes, or cheques, or they can pay by all kinds of bank cards. They can even pay by account. They say, "Put that to my account. I'll not pay now, but you send me an account later and I will pay it then." When money is sent the account is receipted. Look at these which I have here. This one says, PAID IN FULL WITH THANKS. This one - RECEIVED PAYMENT. This just - PAID WITH THANKS. So, these receipts were given because all the accounts were paid.

We are all debtors. What is a debtor? A debtor is someone who owes something. If I did not pay, people would say, "You did not pay your account. You are a debtor. You have not paid what you owe." *We are all debtors to God.* God has presented His account to us. There are ten items on it: the Ten Commandments. He says, "Here, that has to be paid. You have sinned against Me on ten points. That account has to be paid."

You say, "I could never pay that. I am not perfect. I am a sinner and I make mistakes. I do wrong things and I do bad things. I cannot pay that account. What am I going to do?"

God says," You have done things you should not have done, and you have not done things you should have done. When are you going to pay?"

"I cannot pay."

Who is going to pay? The hymn tells us that there

was only One who was good enough to pay the price of sin. Who?

"Jesus."

Yes, it was Jesus who paid the price of our sin. He says that when we are presented with this account from God - all the ten points - He says, "Give it to Me. It will be nailed on My cross with Me. I will write on it in red with My blood, PAID."

Isn't that wonderful? He pays all our debts, and we go free to be His loving children. Isn't that beautiful? Oh, it is the most beautiful and most wonderful thing in the whole, wide world.

> I lay my sins on Jesus,
>   The spotless Lamb of God;
> He bears them all, and frees us
>   From the accursed load.
> I bring my guilt to Jesus,
>   To wash my crimson stains
> White in His blood most precious,
>   Till not a spot remains.
>
> I lay my wants on Jesus;
>   All fulness dwells in Him;
> He heals all my diseases,
>   He doth my soul redeem.
> I lay my griefs on Jesus,
>   My burdens, and my cares;
> He from them all releases,
>   He all my sorrows shares.

(d) No other way
(Acts 4:12)

I want to tell you a very serious story. It is about how God planned to save us from our sins. God's law says, "The soul that sins, it shall die." That is, if you steal, or swear, tell a lie, be cruel, unkind, selfish, anything bad, you are sinning and, "The soul that sins shall die." God did not wish us to die because He loved us. So He searched for a way to save us from our sins that we would not die.

Jesus Christ, His Son said, "Father, I am willing to die for the people's sins."

His Father might have said, "But My Son, I could not kill You."

Said the Son, "Father, it is the only way because there is nobody else good enough."

You see, if a sinner like you or I died for sins we would only be dying for our own sins. We could not die for anyone else's sins. The only one who could die for anyone else's sins would have to be somebody so good that he had never sinned.

Then Jesus said, "There is no other way than that I die for the people's sins."

God said, "I can't kill You Son. I cannot kill You."

"Ah," said the Son, "I know a way. If you send Me down to earth as a baby, a boy and a man, I know someone who will kill Me. You will not need to do it, Father. Satan will kill Me. Father, if You let him kill Me, he won't be able to keep Me dead because I will not have sinned Myself. You can raise Me on the third day. I will be safe, and Your children will be too, because I will have died for them, on their behalf."

That is what He did and now we can be saved from our sins. God could not kill His Son, but He allowed the Jews and Romans through Satan to do so. But God raised Him on the third day. Boys and girls, Satan is God's servant: he does not want to be that because he hates God, but he can't help it. God used him, and now Jesus can save us from our sins.

> We sing the praise of Him who died,
>   Of Him who died upon the Cross :
> The sinner's hope let men deride,
>   For this we count the world but loss.

> Inscribed upon the Cross we see,
>   In shining letters, "God is love";
> He bears our sins upon the Tree;
>   He brings us mercy from above.

> The Cross! it takes our guilt away;
>   It holds the fainting spirit up;
> It cheers away the gloomy day,
>   And sweetens every bitter cup;

> It makes the coward spirit brave,
>   And nerves the feeble arm for fight;
> It takes the terror from the grave,
>   And gilds the bed of death with light;

> The balm of life, the cure of woe,
>   The measure and the pledge of love,
> The sinner's refuge here below,
>   The angels' theme in heaven above.

(e)Really sorry
(Matthew 21:28-31)

A farmer had two sons. They were grown-up boys. The father was a grape farmer, and one day he sent his sons to the vineyard where the grapes grew. One son said, "Yes, father, I will go" - but he did not. The other one said, "No, I will not go" - but he did. Isn't that funny? One said, "I'll go," and didn't, and the other, "I won't," but he did.

Well now, the one who said he would and didn't go - I wonder what the father thought of him? I suppose he wasn't pleased at the other boy who said, "No, I will not go." But when he saw he had gone, he would have been pleased, wouldn't he? But this one who promised to go then didn't, surely the father would be very grieved with him? He might have taken him aside and said, "Here, young man, what is the meaning of this? You said you would go and you did not." I suppose the son was ashamed when his father spoke to him. He would be sorry.

But why should he be sorry? There are two reasons why the young man might be sorry. The first one is: he might be sorry that he was found out - not sorry that he did not go and work in his father's vineyard, but sorry that he was found out. This first kind of sorrow is remorse. The other kind of sorrow is repentance. Now, if he had been sorry that he disobeyed his father, sorry that he had told a lie - that he said he would go and he didn't - that would be different, that would be repentance.

God is pleased when people repent when they have grieved someone, or grieved God Himself; but when they are only sorry that they are found out, that doesn't please Him because He knows they are not really sorry deep down, sorry that they have grieved their Father in heaven. They are only sorry that they have been found out.

There is a difference between being sorry when you are found out and being sorry because you have done wrong. We used to sing this long ago:

With a sorrow for sin, must repentance begin,
  Then salvation, of course will draw nigh,
But till washed in the blood of the crucified Lord,
  You will never be ready to die.

Will you remember the difference? That when you have done wrong and you are found out, you have to be sorry, not only that you were found out, but that you have done wrong and grieved Mummy, or Daddy, or the Lord. When we do wrong Mummy may weep, and Daddy too; but Jesus in heaven is even more sorry, because He wants us to do right.

Section Two

Teaching Children About Jesus

It is surely one of the loveliest things in the world to teach children about Jesus because their innocence takes to Him at once.

(1) His Life

(a) Flight into Egypt
(Matthew 2)

When Jesus came to earth it was a surprise to most people. Even the shepherds were only told by the angels when it happened. But there was an old man Simeon and an old woman Anna who were sure God's Son would be born then. Mary and Joseph knew, of course, because the angel Gabriel had told them.

But some others knew. We have been reading about them this morning: The Wise Men or Magi (not magicians but great men from the East, probably from Persia). They, apparently were looking for a King of the Jews to be born. When they saw His star rising in the sky, they followed it to Judea. So they went to the present king whose name was Herod, to ask where this King would be born. It surely was not very wise of them to go to the reigning king and say, "Where is the One who is born to take your place as king?"

"Who thinks he is going to take my place?" thought Herod. "There is no other king of the Jews going to grow up in this land but him I choose to succeed me when I die." Herod had been so frightened that someone would seize his throne that he killed two of his sons and their mother, then a third son. He was cruel because he was scared. So when Herod heard of a King of the Jews being born, he was determined that He must be killed also. What do you think he did? He told the wise men to come back and tell him when they had found the baby.

"For," he said, "I will go and worship Him also." But what he really meant to do was to send someone to kill the baby. But the Wise Men, after they had seen baby Jesus and given Him their gifts of gold, frankincense and myrrh, were warned by God not to go back to Herod. They went home another way.

When they did not return to Herod, he was so angry, that instead of sending someone straightaway to Bethlehem to find the Baby and kill Him, he said to his soldiers, "Go and kill all the baby boys up to the age of two." What a wicked thing to do! He would have killed all the baby boys up to the age of two years in the hope that the baby King would be among them. Baby Jesus would have been killed if God had not told Joseph to flee to Egypt with the young child.

All the babies up to the age of two were taken from their mothers' arms and slain with the sword before their mothers' eyes. God was very angry with Herod, and he died of a horrible disease. But the baby Jesus was saved and stayed in Egypt till that cruel king had died.

Then Joseph and Mary brought Jesus up from Egypt. But because a son of Herod was king, they did not take him back to Bethlehem, where Jesus was born, but to where they had lived before, a little highland village called Nazareth. Jesus was safe.

So, boys and girls, when wicked men plan and plot to do evil things, as Herod did when he tried to kill God's own Son, God who lives in heaven (which I like to call "upstairs") is looking down, watching. He used to warn people, as He did Joseph, by dreams, but now He warns them by His Word, the Bible, or by His Spirit in men's hearts. He tells us what to do to escape Satan's power. That is why we must live so close to God. He is watching overhead to protect us from evil. That is why we pray to Him.

Loving Shepherd of Thy sheep,
Keep me Lord in safety keep,
Nothing can Thy power withstand,
None can pluck me from Thy hand.

Loving Shepherd, Thou didst give
Thine own life that I might live;
May I love Thee day by day,
Gladly Thy sweet will obey.

Loving Shepherd, ever near,
Teach me still Thy voice to hear;
Suffer not my feet to stray
From the straight and narrow way.

Where Thou leadest may I go,
Walking in Thy steps below;
Then before Thy Father's throne,
Jesus, claim me for Thine own.

(b) The Boy in the Temple
(Luke 2:41-52)

Boys and girls, remember I spoke to you about how people turn Holy Days, like Christmas and Easter, into holidays and, simply forgetting God altogether, go out to enjoy themselves without any thought of Him at all?

Today, I want to tell you about a boy who was a bit older than most of you. He was twelve and was taken from the highlands of Galilee, near where the lake is, to Jerusalem, for probably His first Holy Day with His parents. I think that already most of you have guessed that His name is Jesus. It was at the time of the Passover, about our Easter time.

Jesus was taken to Jerusalem at the age of twelve, because when He was thirteen He would be regarded as a man and would have to keep the law of Moses as an adult. I suppose that Mary and Joseph would have said to Him, "Jesus, this is going to be an exciting visit. All the young folk of Your age will be there. But it is not really a holiday. We are to be there for seven holy days."

Jesus remembered that, and so, when some of the others were perhaps away having fun, or playing games, Jesus went on His own to the temple. There the scholars were sitting around discussing the law of Moses, with some asking questions, others giving answers. The boy Jesus listened, and then because God had given Him a great understanding of God's Word and law, He began to ask questions. (You can read from Matthew 5:21 onwards some of the questions He may have asked.) When these scholars could not give Jesus

the answers He wanted, He gave them His answers.
All the scholars were astonished at how much He
knew about their holy law. This continued past the
time the people from Galilee left to return home.
Mary and Joseph thought that Jesus was with the
other young people who did not want to be always
with their parents. So they went off home, a journey
of three or four days .

The first night, when the caravan (that's what a
crowd of people travelling together is called)
camped for the night, Jesus was not there.

Next morning Mary and Joseph travelled twenty
miles back to Jerusalem. When they got there that
evening there was Jesus, still sitting with the scholars, asking questions and giving answers which astonished them all. Mary said to Him, "Why have
You done this to us, son? Your father and I have
been anxiously searching for You, wondering what
had become of You." Do you know what Jesus
answered? He said, "Why were you searching for
Me? Did you not know that I had to be about My
Father's business in His house (that is the temple)?"

Do you see what Jesus meant? He was saying to
Mary, " Mother, you know that Joseph is not really
My father, except on paper in the Jewish register
book. God is My Father. I have to be in His house,
not in Joseph's house, doing My Father in heaven's
will." Wasn't that wonderful for a boy of twelve?
But Jesus,being a perfectly obedient boy, went home
with Mary and Joseph. He stayed with them until
He was thirty; some people think Joseph may have
died before then and Jesus stayed until His brothers
grew up, making His living at carpentry for them
and for Mary. Isn't that a beautiful story, and true?

(c)Jesus' Baptism
(Matthew 3:13-17)

Boys and girls, I want to tell you what I thought was a "riddle" but it is really a puzzle! There are puzzles that you can solve with your hands, others like crosswords where you have to use your heads.

A riddle is a short saying with a question, and the answer has to be thought out, because it is hidden. For instance, in the Bible, Samson gave ("propounded" is the word) a riddle to the Philistines: "Out of the strong came forth sweetness." Another line of it said, "Out of the eater, came forth meat."

Let us take the first part: "Out of the strong came forth sweetness." Do you know what that meant? Well, Samson was a strong man. He had killed a lion with his bare hands. Later, when he passed by the place where the lion lay dead he found some wild bees had made their home in the lion's carcase - its dead body. "Out of the strong came forth sweetness." You see the second part too, "Out of the eater (that is the lion) came forth meat (food - honey)."

But of course the riddle has a deeper meaning. The strong could be God, who for all His power, is wonderfully sweet, and kind, gentle and loving.

Now, the riddle or puzzle I have for you today is in what we read in the Bible. It is simply this: Jesus came to John the Baptist at the river Jordan to be baptised. John said to Jesus, "Oh no, cousin, I should be baptised by You." Why did Jesus want to be baptised by John? Why did John say that it was he, John, who should be baptised by Jesus?

First of all, what is Baptism? It has to do with

water. Baptism is dipping people in water, or pouring, or sprinkling water on them. But why do that? There is a sense in which we "baptise" ourselves every day - or when we are small someone does it for us, because we wash ourselves with water! We also drink it - not the same water, but clean water. Water is life. We can't live without water. We can live for a long time without food, although if it was too long a time we would die; but we need water to drink. A good part of our body is made up of water.

Just as water is used for washing our bodies clean, so it is used in baptism to picture that the water of life, which is Jesus' Spirit, also washes our souls clean from sin. But why then baptise Jesus since He never sinned as a boy or as a man? John was surely right when he said, "Oh no, cousin Jesus, I should not baptise You, but You me." But Jesus said, "It is right, cousin John, for Me to be baptised!" Jesus insisted, so John baptised Him.

What did Jesus mean? Why was it right for Jesus to be baptised, although He was not a sinner and had never sinned? It was because He came to bear all our sins on the Cross. When people accused Jesus of being a sinner, He did not open His mouth to defend Himself. He did not deny it and say He was not a sinner, because He was to die as *the Sinner*. He was bearing the punishment for all our sins.

I have sometimes called Jesus, "God's Criminal", because He died as if He had been the only sinner in the world. I have also called Him, "God's Dustman". You know what a dustman is? He is someone who takes away other people's dirt. If you sit next to a dustman on the bus, and you see how dirty his clothes are, remember it is not his own dust on his clothes but that of other people. He bears away their dirt. That is what Jesus did. Only a sinless man could do that - bear away our dirty sins. If a sinner tried to die for the sins of others, he would simply die for his own, and could not die for anyone else's; he would go to hell.

Now, never forget that: that is one of the most important things you should know in the whole world. Jesus died our death for sin, that we should live with Him, for ever.

(d)His Temptation
(Matthew 4:1-11)

Jesus was tempted by the devil three times in the desert. The first time, Satan tempted Him to turn stones into bread, because He must have been very hungry after forty days and nights without food.

The second temptation was, that Jesus should throw Himself down from the top of the temple. Satan said the Father's angels would catch Him, and people would see what a wonderful person He was, and believe in Him. But of course if Jesus had done that and had obeyed the devil, he would have had Him in his power and he would have destroyed Him.

The third temptation was to take Him to a very high mountain and show Him all the world that Satan was once given to rule as God's assistant. He would say to Jesus, "I will give it all to You, if You will fall down and worship me." But Jesus would not do that. He answered the devil each time with a text from the Scriptures. Satan can't stand Scripture, except when he leaves bits out of it and takes away its meaning and power. So Satan gave up on Jesus. Then God's angels came and looked after the hungry, thirsty Jesus. He was soon all right again.

It is the first temptation I want to speak to you about, the temptation to turn stones into bread. Before this, after Jesus' baptism by John the Baptist, God's dove of peace had come down on Jesus when God's voice from heaven had said, "This is My Son whom I love; I am well pleased with Him." God the Father meant that He was pleased with Jesus for being willing to be baptised and take our

place and be punished for our sins on the Cross.
That is why Jesus came: to die for our sins. It was
after His baptism that Jesus was led by the Spirit
into the wilderness to be tempted by the devil.
How he tempted Jesus for forty days and forty
nights we don't know. But he waited all that long
time when Jesus had no food or drink, before he
said, "If You are the Son of God, tell these stones
to become bread, for You can work miracles."

Now, that might have seemed a good idea, but
not when Satan said it. It would have given him
power over Jesus. He would have been able to say,
"I told Jesus what to do, and He did it." He would
have gone on ordering Jesus about until he would
have destroyed Him. That is what the devil wanted
to do. He was mad that Jesus was God and he was
just a creature whom God had made. He knew that
he could never be God. Jesus then took up another
kind of stone (the Bible calls its texts "rocks") from
Deuteronomy 8:3 and hurled it at Satan. He said,
"Man shall not live by bread alone but by every word
that comes out of the mouth of God." If Jesus had
turned the stones in the wilderness into bread He
would have been living, not by God's words, but by
Satan's. That would have been awful, wouldn't it?

Why did Satan wait forty days and forty nights
before he came with that temptation? He waited
until Jesus was weak due to lack of food. What a
nasty, wicked creature Satan is; he waits until we
are weak and weary before he attacks us in the
strongest way he can. Because he is a horrid foe, he
loves to get us when we are down - down with
sickness, or tiredness, or something like that. Then
he comes at us. We have to watch and ask God not

to let us be led into temptation but to rescue us from the evil one. We say that in the Lord's Prayer: "Lead us not into temptation, but deliver us from evil."

Sometimes he comes gliding in like an angel of light and speaks to us as if he were God; other times he comes at us like a roaring lion and frightens us out of our wits. Then we must run to Jesus and ask Him to protect us from Satan because we are weak and not able to face him. And Jesus will. Paul says we are never tempted beyond what we can stand. We need to send up a sky-telegram to God. You know what that is? It is a quick cry, "Oh God, help me, Satan is creeping up to me." Or, "Satan has nearly bowled me over. Come quickly and help."

That is what Jesus did in the Garden before He was arrested. He prayed, the Bible says, until His sweat came like drops of blood. But God sent an angel to strengthen Him. He will send an angel to strengthen you too. You'll not see the angel, but he will come, like God's invisible Spirit. He will be there to strengthen you, and give you a rock of Scripture to throw at the devil, as Jesus did.

(e)His Transfiguration
(Matthew17:1-13)

I want to speak to you today about what we read
in the Bible, of Jesus going up a high mountain. I
think it was the one I visited when I went to Israel,
where, on the top, I saw a church dedicated to
Moses and Elijah. It is dedicated to them because
people believe it was there that they appeared to
Jesus, our Lord, before His three disciples, Peter,
James and John. The Bible says something happened to Jesus while He was there. He suddenly
began to shine very brightly, as if His body and His
clothes were all lit up. The Bible says He glistened.
Then God's voice thundered from heaven to say to
the three disciples, that although it was wonderful
to have Moses and Elijah appear because they
had been dead for hundreds of years, a greater
than Moses or Elijah was there. Jesus is God's only
begotten Son, and they were to hear Him, rather
than listen to Moses or Elijah.

But what about Jesus all lit up? There are two
ways of lighting up; you can have light from the
inside or from the outside. Inside, you might switch
on the light in the room, but from outside a policeman or a burglar could shine his torch into the room
and it would be lit up that way. You see the difference? One shines from within, the other from without.

Now here is your question. When Jesus was lit up
on the mountain, did the light shine on Him or from
Him? Did it shine as it shone on Saul of Tarsus
when he was stopped on the Damascus road by a
light from heaven brighter than the noonday sun, so

bright that it blinded him for a day or two? Or was the light shining within Jesus, shining out from Him? I believe it was a light which shone out from inside Jesus. God wanted to let us see how beautiful and wonderful Jesus' heart and mind were. What a lovely, kind, good, honest and true man Jesus was inside.

Sometimes we can dress up to look different from what we really are; a comedian, or a clown can put on a wig, or a beard and funny clothes to make himself look quite different. Just the same way, we can put on smiles (or are they grins?) which make us look nice outside so that people might say, "He is such a nice, little boy" or "She is such a sweet, little girl." But Mummy or Daddy may be saying to themselves, "Yes, but you should see their other face, when they are in a temper, or refusing to do what they are told, or saying something nasty, or fighting with other children. You would see that they are not always as nice inside as that sweet smile seems to be saying."

But the great thing about Jesus is, that Jesus was as nice inside as He was outside, specially to children. He loved to play with children and gather them round, putting His arms round them, especially if they were sick or sad little ones. So, when God the Father switched on the light, which was in Jesus' heart and mind, it was seen that He was far more beautiful, and wonderful, and good, and kind, and true than people would see simply by looking at Him in the street.

It was just for a moment that God the Father allowed the three disciples, Peter, James and John to see Jesus lit up. He gave what we might say was a preview of His glory, to show how beautiful He is inside. But one day, when Jesus comes back in power and glory, He is going to light us all up like that. I wonder when He comes and we get our new resurrection bodies, will we shine like Jesus? The reason Jesus shone was because God's Spirit was in His heart, making Him beautiful. It is God's Spirit dwelling in us who is going to make us shine when Jesus comes to give us new bodies and switch on our lights for us to shine in glory.

O wondrous type, O vision fair
Of glory that the Church shall share,
Which Christ upon the mountain shows,
Where brighter than the sun He glows!

With shining face and bright array,
Christ deigns to manifest to-day
What glory shall be theirs above,
Who joy in God with perfect love.

(2) His Parables

(a) Parable of the Pounds
(Luke 19:11-27)

I want to speak about a story from the New Testament that Jesus told. It was really about Himself: this is how He started it. A certain nobleman (a grand man) went one day to a far country so that he might become a king and then return. Who did He mean by that? It was Himself. It was Jesus who was going to heaven to be made King because He had gained the victory over all bad things on the Cross. He went to heaven for His Father to make Him the King - King of kings and Lord of lords. Then He would return. It is a long time since He went there - nearly 2,000 years. He has not returned yet, but He is coming back.

Before this king left he took his ten servants aside, and giving to each one of them a pound said, "Now use that and see how much profit you can gain before I come back."

So, when He came back (Jesus is imagining that He has come back, although He hasn't really yet) He saw one of His servants and said, "How much have you gained from your pound?"

"Oh," he said, "I have gained ten pounds." And do you know what Jesus meant in His reply to him? "When you get to heaven I am going to make you lord over ten cities (like a Lord Mayor)." We will be very busy in heaven. Some think they are going to heaven to sleep and never do anything but fold their arms. We are going to work very hard there, but will be able to because we will have new bodies.

Then He said to another one, "How much have you gained?"

"Five pounds."

"Oh well, I'll put you in charge of five cities once you get to heaven." Heavenly cities - I wonder what they will be like.

Then He came to another and asked, "How much have you gained for your pound?" He hung his head and said, "Nothing. I think You are a hard man and I have gained nothing from my pound." So, there was nothing said to him about going to heaven for he wouldn't be there because he didn't like Jesus. (Nobody will go to heaven who doesn't like Jesus. How can they? Would Jesus allow people into His house who don't like Him and who hate Him? Never!) So he didn't get to heaven.

Now, when we become Jesus-children and Jesus-people, Jesus gives us all power to serve, even when we are very small. As soon as we can understand and love Jesus, Jesus gives to us who love Him, the tiniest as well as the biggest, the power to serve. Later on, when you grow up some will be made elders and deacons, others will serve the church as organists, church-officers, printers, treasurers, cleaners in the church, people who visit the parish and evangelists. But while you are small you can't be elders, or deacons, or any of those things. But you can still serve the Lord Jesus, though you are young and quite small.

Sometimes after a service when I see James running around with his sleeves up, gathering all the hymn books that people have left in their seats, heaps of them to be taken to the vestibule, I think, would no one in the congregation help him to do that? I remember when there used to be lots of little boys who helped James to do that. That would be one way to help the Lord Jesus. Then there is helping to set the chairs right when people move them around. Help Mummy and Daddy at home too. At school, offer to help teacher and also your friends. Speak to them, not only about Sunday School and Church but about Jesus. Ask them if they know about Jesus, if they love Him. Lots of little boys and girls in days past have brought their friends to Church and they have learned about Jesus and begun to love Him.

In a home, where all the people serve Jesus: Mummy by doing all that she has to do, Daddy by going out to business or whatever, the children by helping one another; the whole family help and take their proper place, doing their bit, and are happy because they are working together, seeking to do good by God's help and loving Jesus. If that is the case and we seek to serve Jesus with all our might, then when we get to heaven I think we will be busier because He is going to give us more to do. But then we will be able for it. We will enjoy it because all the work in heaven will be lovely work. It will be very, very pleasant.

All right then, will you remember that God gives His children power to serve Him all their lives? It is amazing what some very old people can do to serve Jesus. Indeed, some of the best work that people have done in their whole lives has been when they are not able to get out and they may sit at the fireside, or lie in bed, and they pray to the Lord Jesus for His Church. Some pray for us. That is perhaps the greatest thing they can do. Wonderful!

(b) The Ten Bridesmaids
(Matthew 25:1-13)

Have any of you ever been bridesmaids, or flower girls? None of you here? Oh, what a pity. If you were asked to be one, what would you carry in your hand? Yes, flowers - a posy of flowers. But the bridesmaids we were reading about today didn't carry any flowers at all. Were you listening? What did they carry? They carried lamps. What would you think if you saw a wedding in Aberdeen with the bridesmaids carrying lamps? But then, what kind of lamps? Not torches with batteries; they didn't have such in those days. The lamps they had were little dishes with a lip like this one. But the dish part would have been full of oil and there would have been a wick. Every candle has a wick to make it burn. Candles today burn wax, long ago they burned oil. You know that wax becomes like oil when it is melted. It burns as long as the oil comes along the wick, and that gives the light. See! That is the kind of light they were carrying. Some had jars as well so that when the oil burned up they would put in more.

Here are pictures of the kind of lamps they had. Look at them. They each have a different number of lips so that this has four wicks coming out, which would give four lights. Another one has seven. In Zechariah 4:2 we read of a lamp with seven wicks - the perfect number seven, with seven lights. Lamps were made of pottery or of metal.

That is the kind of lamps the bridesmaids would carry. Ten bridesmaids - what a retinue that would be! What a procession! Ten bridesmaids all with their lamps. Five brought a jar with oil to fill up when the oil went done, but five didn't. When the bridegroom came and the lights were growing dim and going out,they said, "The bridegroom is a long time coming, we didn't think he would be so long." He was such a long time coming that their lamps went out. Turning to the wise bridesmaids they said, "Give us some oil out of your jars."

"No," said the other girls. "If we did that there would not be enough for us to light our lamps when we go to meet the bridegroom."

Now, I wonder what all this means? Five had oil so that their lamps would not go out, and five had not enough oil and their lamps did go out. I suppose, as bridesmaids look pretty when they come down the aisle of the Church with these lovely bouquets of flowers, so these bridesmaids would come forward with their lights to welcome the bridegroom. This shows that when Jesus comes it will be an awful thing for our light to go out. There was a bride once here and she forgot something very important. In the excitement of dressing and getting out to the car, she forgot her bouquet and someone had to rush home for it. If the bridesmaids in the story came out to meet the bridegroom and the light had gone out - that would be sad. What it means is this, that when Jesus comes, we must see that our lights are shining. Our lights only keep shining when we have oil in our lamps. Oil stands for Jesus in our hearts. If we have Jesus in our hearts He will take us in to the wedding.

Did you know that there is going to be a wedding in heaven? The Church will be married to Jesus, the Bridegroom. Isn't that marvellous?

(c) The Lost Sheep
(Matthew 18:10-14)

Children, we are to think about sheep today, lots
of them - a hundred sheep in fact. If you were riding
in a car and you came upon a flock of a hundred
sheep, with a shepherd and two dogs, it would take
quite a time for you to pass them and see that none
of them was hurt. I was once driving from Aultbea
when, suddenly, a sheep ran into the middle of the
road, and met the full force of my car's front tyre.
There it lay. There was no flock; it was on its own.
I couldn't believe that it was dead, but it was. The
owner came along and I got out to say how sorry I
was. He said, "Well!" and dragged the animal to
the side of the road. Maybe it was one of a hundred
and the shepherd had lost it. I always think of that,
when I read the story of Jesus' hundred sheep, and
the one, lost. It was not dead, but away in the hills,
as the hymn says 'far from its home'.

I was surprised that the sheep farmer was not
more angry with me for having killed his sheep. As I
looked at the poor, dead beast, I thought he should
have been more angry, because it had been killed by
my car. If I had been going still slower - I was not
going fast because I was on a side road - it might still
have been alive. Now, if that sheep had, when it
was young, been a special little lamb of the farmer's
daughter, which she had fed with a bottle, then she
would have been broken-hearted. But the farmer
just said, "Well!" I wanted to pay for the sheep but
he waved his hand and said, "No, no." Off I drove,
feeling almost like a murderer.

It was different with Jesus' shepherd, that we

read of in the Bible. If someone had said to him when one of his sheep got lost, "Och, it doesn't matter for one sheep, when you've still got ninety-nine", he would have said, "But I love every one of my sheep; they've all got names. They're almost like children to me; I can't just leave this one, (calling it by its name - let's say it was "Zechariah") I can't just let Zechariah go astray like that and not care! I must leave all these ninety-nine, and go and look for the one lost sheep."

Out to the hills the shepherd would go - over moors, up hills, down dales and over steep crags, crying as he went, "Zechariah - Zechariah - Where are you?" He was thinking, "Are you hurt, or just not caring because you have come to some nice, green grass, in a dangerous place?" Because he loved it he would climb and scramble and tire himself out looking for that lost sheep. The ninety-nine at home in the sheepfold were safe so they didn't matter at all then. All that he could think of was his one lost sheep, Zechariah.

Boys and girls, Jesus tells us that God loves us like that. If all His children were safe in His heavenly sheepfold, except for one little lamb, His heart would be breaking, and He would say, "I can't rest until that little lamb of Mine is found. Poor little thing; I wonder where it is, and how it is. It may be hurt; I must go and find it, and bring it back home." That is how God loves us. He loves us individually, which means that if all His children in the whole, wide world were all safe, and just you were lost, He would break His heart for you, and turn His whole world upside down until He found you. He cares for you so much, that if you had been the only lost

lamb in the world He would have sent His Son,
Jesus, to die for you. Think of that! You are as much
to Him, as if you were the only one that had to be
died for. He would have been prepared to send
His Son to the Cross, just to save you only. Isn't
that wonderful love?

We are going to sing about it in a great hymn:

There were ninety and nine that safely lay
In the shelter of the fold;
But one was out on the hills away,
Far off from the gates of gold;
Away on the mountains wild and bare,
Away from the tender Shepherd's care.

But none of the ransomed ever knew
How deep were the waters crossed,
Nor how dark was the night that the Lord passed
through,
Ere He found the sheep that was lost.
Out in the desert He heard its cry,
Sick and helpless and ready to die.

And all through the mountains, thunder-riven,
And up from the rocky steep,
There rose a cry to the gate of heaven,
'Rejoice I have found My sheep.'
And the angels echoed around the throne,
'Rejoice, for the Lord brings back His own.'

(d)The Brazen Serpent
(Numbers 21 & John 3:14-15)

We have been thinking of Israel marching for forty years through the desert from Egypt to Canaan. During that long period the Israelites often complained. At one point they complained to Moses and Aaron about food, and God gave them manna and also quails (little birds) to eat. Later on they complained because there was not any water. Then they complained about something else and God sent fire amongst them and burned some of them. Still later they refused to go up into Canaan and they blamed Moses and Aaron again for taking them out of Egypt. They said they would rather go back to Egypt to be slaves than die in the wilderness.

Then this last time they complained again about water. Moses was very angry with them and struck the rock so that the water came out. But they not only blamed Moses for their troubles, they blamed God. They sinned against God who had rescued them from Egypt and had looked after them for nearly forty years through the wilderness. They spoke against God and He was very, very angry. So, He sent poisonous snakes among them. These snakes bit them, and many died.

Then they were sorry. They were always sorry when they had sinned and brought trouble on themselves. "Oh, we are sorry, Moses, speak to God for us." Moses spoke to God and the Lord said, "Make a brass serpent and put it on a pole. Everyone who has been bitten by a snake and is dying from the bite will be healed, if he looks at the brass snake."

Now, that is a strange thing, isn't it - a brass snake? They were to look to the brass snake, and they would be healed of the snake bites. But stranger than that, Jesus referred to this incident. We read of it in John's Gospel. He said that the brass snake stands for Him. We know that Satan is a serpent and these were horrid serpents that bit the people. God allowed Satan to send them to bite the people to punish them because He was angry with them. But Jesus says *that the brass snake stands for Him:* "As Moses lifted up the serpent in the wilderness, and those who had been bitten by the snakes were healed when they looked at the brass serpent, so all who look to Me on the Cross will be saved."

Now, why did Jesus say that? Have you any ideas? It is very difficult: Jesus likening Himself to a brass snake! Well, I will tell you what I think, and what lots of other people have thought, it may mean. The brass snake stands for Jesus bearing the punishment of our sins. Brass is said in the Old Testament to represent punishment and judgment. It seems that that is what it must mean: Jesus was lifted up on the Cross to bear the punishment for our sins, so that we may go free and be healed and be with Him forever in glory. Isn't that marvellous? Isn't that astonishing that Jesus said that, "As Moses lifted up the serpent, so if I am lifted up on the Cross those that look to Me will be saved?"

We know we can only be saved by Jesus, because He took our punishment for our sins. He bore our punishment so that we could go free. Wonderful! Wonderful! Wonderful Gospel story! NEVER FORGET IT.

(3) His Miracles

(a)1,000 to a bun
(Matthew14:13-21)

We were reading about Jesus feeding five thousand men. I wonder how many women were there, and children with them. There could have been over seven thousand people altogether. They had gone to a place very difficult to get to. It could not have been easy for women and children to go there. But they were seeking healing for their bodies which is why they had hurried round to the other side of the Lake of Galilee to be with Jesus.

What food had they? Yes, they had five loaves, or buns as I would call them and two fishes. Five buns to five thousand or more people! Arithmetic lesson: how many people to a bun? 1,000 of course. A thousand people to a bun! Now, I have here this bun. The little boy we read of had five like this and two fish. Jesus took the boy's lunch and looked up to heaven and prayed. He thanked God. Did He thank God for the five buns and two fish? I will be telling the big folks later on that I think He was also thanking His Father for what He was going to do. For it is God the Father who performs all miracles. After He thanked God, He began to divide the buns into little bits.

Would you like a little bit of this bun? Come on, it won't bite you - you bite it. There we are. What if I had to feed a thousand from this one bun. I have only given you tiny bits of this bun but already it is beginning to look small. Do you think I could feed all the congregation? Oh no! I might manage this row of people, maybe that row, but then it would be done *unless* I also were to ask our Father in heaven to multiply it because people were very hungry and they needed food.

How did God the Father do this? What happened? Jesus took bits off and bits off and yet there were more and more bits. How was it done? Do you know? Anybody here, the eldest and the wisest, know how it was done? We don't know. We don't know how it was done at all because it was a pure miracle. God the Father in heaven did something to the bread and fish so that everyone - and this is the astonishing thing - was satisfied. I just give you tiny nibbles which would never have fed a hungry man, not even a hungry little gir. I think Jesus gave them large pieces. If I had broken this bun into four or five large pieces it would have been finished. I wonder how it happened. Isn't it marvellous what God did with bread, just because the people were hungry. It is a marvellous story, isn't it? It is absolutely wonderful. I'm afraid I can't do the same with an Aberdeen "morning rowie" (roll).

(b)The Centurion's Servant
(Matthew 8:5-13)

We have read about a centurion. A centurion was an officer in the Roman army who had command of a hundred soldiers. He commanded them to go and they went, to come and they came, and so on. Now this centurion's servant (his boy, or batman or valet) was very, very sick. He was "sick of the palsy" as the Bible says. His master wanted him to be well. So he came to Jesus and told Him about him. Jesus said, "I will come and heal him." That was what He had done to the leper who had said, "If You will, You could cure my disease of leprosy."

The centurion said, "My servant is sick."

Immediately Jesus said, "I will come and heal him." He was always willing to help.

"Oh no," said the centurion looking at Jesus and recalling some of His wonderful teaching and His healing of sick people. He had a great respect for Jesus. "Oh no," he said, "You can't come to my house." I expect he had a very nice house because he was an officer in the army. "Oh no, I wouldn't let You come to my poor house. I wouldn't think of it. You are far too great and good and wonderful a person to come into my house. I couldn't let You come to my house. Just say the word and my servant will be healed."

Jesus looked at him, and the Bible says He was astonished at the man. "You are saying to Me, where I am standing now - and your house is a mile away - that I just say, where I am, the word about your sick servant being healed and a mile away your servant will be healed? Do you believe that?"

"Yes," said the centurion, "I believe. I believe that You have the power to do this, and You are obviously willing to do it."

Isn't that marvellous faith? That is why Jesus said, "I haven't found faith like that amongst the Jews. I wish the Jews would trust Me like that. I wish they would believe I had the power to do them good. But they don't. These Pharisees and scribes, the important Jews, don't believe in Me; some of them want to kill Me. But you have such trust in Me that you are saying to Me, that standing where I am, I have just to say the word and, away there where your house is, your servant will be healed?"

Jesus said the word. "All right, if that is what you want. You know I don't need to come into your house. But I would like to come. It is no trouble to Me."

"I don't think my house is worthy," said the centurion. "But say the word and my servant will be healed."

And he was healed. When the centurion went home and saw his servant well, he asked what time he began to get better. They counted back. He was healed of his palsy at the exact time that Jesus said he would. Isn't that wonderful? That is how great our Jesus is. He is wonderful, great, powerful and kind. We believe on Him with all our heart, don't we? We believe on Him, trust Him, love Him and ask Him to do wonderful things for us.

(c)Blind Beggars
(Matthew 20:29-34)

I want to talk to you today about the blind beggars we read of in the Bible. They were sitting by the roadside in a very hot place, Jericho. There was a great crowd of people passing by, on their way to Jerusalem for the "Easter" festival, as we might call it. They were going to the Passover feast in Jerusalem, about twenty-five miles up in the hills from Jericho. Jericho is lower than the level of the sea - 1200 feet below the sea. It has the most beautiful flowers, the largest roses I ever saw - the size of cabbages - and beautiful trees with blossom, and water which makes it bright and verdant, green and fresh.

These beggars heard that Jesus was there, perhaps leading the crowd. They had heard about Jesus of Nazareth who did wonderful things - healing cripple people, sick people, deaf people, BLIND people and raising the dead too. They must have nudged one another and said, "Jesus of Nazareth is coming. We are not going to let Him pass. No, no He must attend to us. We want to see. It is all very well to sit here begging for money. Money is all very well but money won't help you to see. We want our sight. He is the man who can give us our sight." So they shouted, and they shouted, and they shouted.

The thing that I don't understand, and it is this I am going to tell you about, is how the very religious people behaved. They were on their way to a religious festival at Jerusalem, to worship God at the Passover feast. They turned to these beggars, when they heard them and said, 'Shut up!' Didn't they know that these men wanted their sight, and that the Man who was leading the crowd could give it to them and help them so that they would not need to beg anymore because they could go out and work and earn wages? I don't suppose there was anybody in those days who could teach the blind to work as they are taught today. Many blind people are very clever and some of them do wonderful work. But in those days they were set aside: even by the crowd going to their religious festival. What do you think of that? I think it is awful. I think it is dreadful. I think it is disgusting. They did not care a rap for those blind men who wanted their sight. That was all the blind men wanted: they just wanted to see like other people. Oh, it is so horrible that religious people can be so hard and callous and nasty. I think it is terrible.

But Jesus heard the chaps shouting. He called them and gave them their sight. What did they do after that? They became pilgrims too, and followed on with the crowd. I wonder if some of the crowd looked down on them. I suppose they had been in rags, poor chaps. Do you think some of the crowd turned up their noses at them? I hope they didn't, because they were going to Jerusalem to worship God. Perhaps because Jesus took so much notice of the blind beggars some of the people in the crowd would have learned a very important lesson about caring for poor, blind and sick people. I hope that we have learned how much Jesus cares for poor, sick, unhappy and lonely people. He often picks out the worst person who is there and says, "Ah, this is the one, not the grand ones all dressed up, the big ones."

Remember Him another time when the children were crowding round Him, the disciples said, "Away, away, away!" "No," said Jesus, "don't push them away. The kingdom of heaven is made up of people like these little children."

We have all to become like little children before we get into heaven. Jesus said, "Don't push them away," and He gathered them around Him. Isn't He lovely? Isn't He beautiful? Isn't He wonderful, our Jesus? We are going to sing about this.

When mothers of Salem
Their children brought to Jesus,
The stern disciples drove them
back and bade them depart;
But Jesus saw them ere they fled,
And sweetly smiled, and kindly said,
'Suffer little children
To come unto Me.'

'For I will receive them
And fold them to My bosom;
I'll be a Shepherd to these lambs,
O drive them not away;
For, if their hearts to Me they give,
They shall with Me in glory live:
Suffer little children
To come unto Me.'

Section Three

Teaching Children About The Bible

How wonderful to show even to little children that the secrets about this marvellous world we live in and about ourselves are hidden in God's Book, the Bible and we are to find them there!

(a) Playing with Food
(1Timothy1:1-11)

I know that you all play with your toys. But I'm afraid lots of children also play with their food. Do you remember, when you were younger and used to sit in a high chair beside the table, what you used to do with your food? You would have your spoon and sometimes you were not very sure where your mouth was and some of your food went on to the crown of your head, or round the back of your neck, or down your bib. Sometimes the plate went on to the floor and an awful mess was made. Mummy had to clean it up - and that was food she had prepared. She had gathered the things that go into it, cooked it and prepared it, put it on your plate, and this is what you did with it: you decorated yourself with it, instead of putting it into your mouth and eating it.

When you get older, how many of you when you go to the table say to Mummy, "What is this? I don't like this. I don't want that. I won't have this." Of course, everybody has their favourite dishes. I have mine. There are some things that we don't like. But we don't eat only because we like what we eat. What would happen to us if we didn't eat at all? We would die. We need to eat food to give us strength, even if we don't like it. Some people when they are sick can't eat food at all and have to be taken to hospital and given food in a special way because if they didn't have food they would die. We need food to make us strong.

It is the same with food for our souls. God's book, the Bible, is food for our souls. It is all good. Mummy would not put anything on to your plate that would poison you, or make you ill, would she? Never! Never! And God has not put anything on our plate that is poison. God's Book from beginning to end is all good. Some people take it up and say, "What is this? I don't agree with this. I like this bit, but I don't like that bit." That is silly of course, because if God has spoken it, we have to take the bits we don't like. If He has written it all down, then we have to take it all because it is food for our souls.

It may be like medicine. When I was a little boy we didn't often have pills, but had to taste some dreadful medicines out of bottles: cascara, castor oil, cod liver oil. HORRID! Now you just put a prettily coloured pill in your mouth and swallow it. But in those days they were nasty medicines but we had to take them because they were good for us. On God's plate there is everything that is good in the Bible for us to eat. We must take it all.

What is your favourite food?

"Ice-cream, chocolate, chips."

But you couldn't eat these all the time. You need other things - fruit, bread, cheese - to make you strong. Just as we must eat all the things which Mummy gives us which are good for us, so we must not pick and choose in God's Word.

Other people like to doctor their food. That means, putting so much salt, or so much sugar on it that it changes the taste. We must not doctor God's food. We must eat it as He has given it to us.

Eat first, not because you like it, but because it is good for you. Will you remember that?

(b) The Seed of God
(1 John 3:3-10)

I want to speak to you for a little this morning about a word we have just read in the Bible. It is the word "seed". Now, the New Testament was first written in the language of the Greeks. The Greeks under Alexander the Great conquered the Holy Land about three hundred years before Jesus was born, and they left their language there. Now, there are two words for seed in the Greek language used in the New Testament: the one we read this morning in 1 John 3:9 is the word *sperma* and the other is written by Peter in 1 Peter 1:23, *sporos*.

You would think that these two words meaning seed, sperma and sporos, spelled out different kinds of seeds because there are different kinds of seeds, aren't there? But these two words don't. Sperma can mean plant seed of corn or a flower, or it can mean seed of an animal. Also sporos can mean plant seed or seed of an animal.

You can see plant seed in packets in a shop with all the colours of the flowers on the packet - lovely flowers that will grow if you plant them properly, feed them with fertiliser and look after them and water them. We say some people have green fingers because they are good at making plants grow, and plants are mostly green. Some people even speak to their plants to make them grow well. But whether you speak to them or not, plants give people great pleasure when they show their different forms and colours. Sometimes you say to yourself when you have planted seeds in the ground, or in a pot and up comes the flower, "Did that flower really come

from that tiny, little seed?" Yes, if you plant them in
the right kind of soil and look after them the tiny
seeds from the packet will grow like the flowers on
the packet.

Now, the seeds of animals are very different and
are very private. They are secretly placed in the
animals' bodies, and the baby animal grows there
from a tiny, tiny living thing till it is ready to be born.
It is wonderful to see a newborn creature.   You
sometimes see them at the zoo, or on the farm, or a
pussy has kittens, or your dog has puppies.

The seed of human beings are planted in the
same way as in animals. They also grow until it is
time for the baby to be born. Isn't it wonderful to
think that you and I were once tiny, little seeds?
Look how we have grown - some of us still growing,
and fast.

Boys and girls, there is another kind of seed, and
it is still the same word, *sperma,* that is used, as in
John's Letter here. It is the seed of God planted
within us, the seed of His Word, the Bible. Now,
think of that: not only is the tiny seed of a human
planted in another human being - and that is a wonderful thing - but the seed of God is also planted in
us. All of us here who love the Lord Jesus have had
that tiny seed of God planted in us. We hope the
seed is growing because that is how we will become
like Jesus.

The only way to become like Jesus is for the
seed of God to grow within us until people begin
to say, "I think that boy, that girl, that man, that
woman is so like Jesus, so kind and true, and strong,
and sweet, and loving. I think they are like what
Jesus was when He was on the earth." That's

lovely, isn't it? That is not surprising for seeds grow like the plants which produce them. We grow like Jesus who plants His seed in our souls by His invisible (unseen) Spirit.

The seed of God needs to be cared for, fed and nourished, just as you have to feed the seed planted in the soil. Animal seeds too need to be fed to make them grow. So, the seed of God within us has to be fed in our souls. Do you know this? I am sure you do, but let me remind you of it. The only food that will make the seed of God grow within us, is God's Word. That is the food that will make us grow. The Bible is the bread of God which we feed on to make us grow like Jesus. We read the Bible to feed on the seed of God until it grows up for people to see Jesus Christ, not only in what we think, but in what we say and in what we do. Isn't that wonderful - the seed of God in our souls growing and being fed by God's Holy Word, helped by His Spirit? I think that is wonderful.

Teaching Children About Prayer

When little ones are taught as they can be readily about the reality of the invisible God and His Presence everywhere but especially where He is loved, prayer becomes the most natural thing in the world.

(a)Asking Prayers
(1 John 5:13-17)

I want to speak to you today about "Asking Prayers". When you pray to God in the name of the Lord Jesus you ask something from Him. How often do you ask? Every day, every night. You ask,"God bless Mummy and Daddy." That would be one of your first prayers, and there would be lots of others. Tell me this: does God always answer your prayers?

"No."

Well, He does, but sometimes the answer is,"No, sorry." I remember, how in the past, when we used to have Sunday School picnics, we used to pray that God would give us a lovely day. Sometimes we had a lovely day, sometimes not a bad day, but sometimes it was raining. We then arranged to go to a church hall. We have been in Inverurie and in Haddo, but you know, when we have had to go into a hall for our picnic and turned it into a party, it was always great fun. So, that although God had said, "No, I am not giving you a nice day for your picnic," it was as if He had said we could still have fun but in a different way. He always knows best, and if you pray and God doesn't answer your prayers, it means He is saying, "Sorry, child." Mummy sometimes says, "Sorry, you can't have that." So God says that sometimes too. It is not because He does not love us. When Mummy says 'No', it is not because she does not love you but because it is not good for you to have what you asked.

Now, at the end of the service you are coming back for the baptism of a little baby girl, a lovely little girl. I am going to tell you about two young people who also had a lovely little girl called Susie. Then they prayed that God would give them a little boy. They prayed that he would be a very fine little boy, the best little boy that ever was. When the little baby was born - and he is being baptised today in another place, down in Southampton - he was not a perfect little boy. He is handicapped. You would know that even by looking at him. Oh, this young Mummy and Daddy have been very sad and sore about this because they had asked and asked of God to give them a proper little boy. But he is not that. There are lots of children like him, but because they may not look right and do not understand things the way you do, Mummies and Daddies and others who know them love them more because they are poor things. Yes, they love them more. So God had a reason for saying, "No, I am not going to give you a proper little boy." He gave them one who would need more and more love from them.

God sometimes says 'No' to our prayers because He has something else in mind. He is planning to do something that we did not think about - like the picnic that turned into a party, and like this little boy who is not quite right so that his Mummy and Daddy will love him all the more. Remember when God does not seem to answer your prayers the way you want, it is not because He does not love you and it is not because He hasn't answered, it is because He has said 'No'. There is something else in His mind for you that you have never thought of, because He is a great, clever and kind God. He knows best.

Sometimes when we pray we say, "Lord, I want this, or I want You to give me that, if it is Your will." Jesus said that when He prayed in the Garden of

Gethsemane. He said, "O Lord, I don't want to go to this Cross." Then He said, "But Father, if it is Your will for Me to go to this Cross, I'll go." And He went. So we have to say that, "If it is Your will, Lord Jesus, give me this or do this for me. If not, just say 'No', and it will be all right."

> Renew my will from day to day;
> Blend it with Thine; and take away
> All that now makes it hard to say
> "Thy will be done."

(b)Ask God First
(Jeremiah 41-42:3)

You believe that God knows everything from the beginning to the end of the world. He knows everyone you are going to meet today before you meet them. He knows how long you are going to live. He knows what you are to become when you grow up - a doctor, or a lawyer, or a nurse, or whatever. He knows everything. He knows how much money you will leave when you die. He knows who you will marry, if you marry. And He knows whether you will have baby boys or baby girls. He knows everything. And because God knows everything we ought to keep very close to Him, which the Jews in Jeremiah's time didn't do. God's people forgot that, and they turned away from Him to other gods . God was very grieved. He was so angry that He said, "Look, you Jews, if you do not turn back to Me, your real God, the only God, then I will send strangers to take you away and make you slaves, captives in another land."

But the Jews wouldn't listen. They would not believe God. Jeremiah, His prophet, reminded them of what God said: "If you do not turn back to Me, I will send you away to Babylon as slaves." But they would not listen. God did send them away to that strange land far, far away.

When the Babylonians came, there were two things that the commander of the army did. He said, "Where is your king, that wicked Zedekiah? Where is he?" And he made him a prisoner, blinded him, and took him away to Babylon. Then he said, "Where is Jeremiah?"

"Oh, Zedekiah took Jeremiah away and put him in prison. He is in prison."

"Well, get him out. We are going to be as kind as we can to Jeremiah because your God told us Jeremiah was saying the same thing as we are saying, that if you do not turn back to your God, we will come and make slaves of you." So, Jeremiah was taken out of prison.

Now, there was a relative of the bad king, a cousin called Ishmael who, when he heard the Babylonians were coming, ran away across the Jordan. When he heard the Babylonians had appointed a governor to rule the people who were left in the land, he said, "I will go and kill him." And he did. He crossed the Jordan back again and killed him near Jerusalem. What did the people do since they had no governor? They didn't know what to do. They went south to Egypt instead of asking God what to do. That was very, very wrong of them. They should have gone to Jeremiah and said, "Oh, we have been very, very bad. God, forgive us and show us what to do." But they didn't. They went on their own and said, "We will go down to Egypt." God did not want them to go down to Egypt. But they didn't ask Him.

This teaches us that when we are going to do anything, we should ask God about it - anywhere you are going, anyone you are going to see, anything you are frightened about - anything at all. You are not very well? Speak to God about it. Speak to God about it *first*. Some people only speak to God when they are in trouble. That is not nice to God, who made us. We should speak to Him all the time. And because He knows everything we should be saying,

"Oh Lord, is this the right way to go? Is this the right thing to do? Is this the right one to speak to?" All the time we should be asking God,"Show me, Lord. You know everything, show me what to do and where to go." They didn't until they were in trouble, but then it was too late.

What do you think we shall sing after that? This is what we shall sing:

Ask the Saviour to help you
Comfort, strengthen and keep you
He is willing to aid you,
He will carry you through.

(c)Victorious prayer
(Revelation 12)

Did you know that Jesus had brothers and sisters? He had a brother called James. He was really a half-brother; Mary was his mother but his father was Joseph. Jesus' Father was God. That made Him different. He was the Son of God.

James wrote a letter about his brother Jesus, whom he called his Saviour and he said in that letter that God was the giver of every good and perfect gift. I want to ask you today to name any good gift that God has given. Don't say, 'Jesus.' We know that He is God's greatest gift. We will leave Him till last because He is the most important. What else?

"Food, clothes, the world, the church, us, hearts."

Yes, but I was thinking of other wonderful things: the sun, the moon, the stars, all the wonders of nature, our friends, and Mummies and Daddies. You wouldn't forget Mummy and Daddy, would you?

We have all these gifts, but the greatest of all is the gift of Jesus to be our Saviour. It is God who gives us all the gifts; Paul says that in Romans 8:32. All the good gifts come through Jesus. But it is a bit like some Christmas presents: some we get without asking for them, and some we get because we ask for them. Is that not so?

Certain gifts that we get from God through Jesus we have to ask for. He wants us to ask for them. That is why we pray. One of the gifts God has given us through Jesus is victory over sin and Satan. When Satan comes and tempts us to think nasty thoughts, to say bad words and to say "No" to

Mummy or Daddy, or to get into a tantrum and make things difficult for Mummy when she is tired, or Daddy when he is busy, then we have this gift that God tells us to ask from Him: the gift of saying "No" to Satan. We say to him when he comes and tempts us to say or do bad things, "Go away in Jesus' name." This is God's gift. This is what God has given to you and to me. This is the gift we were reading of, that God has given to you and to me to say to Satan, "Go away, you rascal. In Jesus' name - scram! Clear out!" And he does because Jesus has gained the victory. He has mastered Satan.

You see the red cross on the pulpit light? Last Sunday a little boy from Sanday in Orkney was asking me, "What is that red cross for?" I said to him, "You don't need to ask me that." And of course he didn't. That red cross stands for Jesus' victory over Satan. It means that Jesus has beaten Satan. So, when we say, "In Jesus' name," Satan retreats and the temptation goes and we don't want to be bad any more. We don't want to say bad things, or think bad thoughts, or do naughty things.

Remember this: whenever you are tempted to be angry-grrr ! you are to say to Satan, for it is he who is making you bad and naughty, "In Jesus' name (I like this word), SCRAM! Scram! Scram Satan!" And he will go and you won't want to be bad anymore.

(d)Daniel

What do you know about Daniel? Yes, he was in the lions' den. The lions didn't eat him up because God shut their mouths. When the king came in early in the morning there was Daniel. He didn't expect to see Daniel at all. Now, do you know why Daniel was put in the lions' den? I will tell you.

Daniel was a very wonderful young man. He belonged to the Jewish royal family. After he was taken captive to Babylon, their king appointed him to a very high position. But some of the people who lived in the land were jealous. They were very jealous because this stranger, this incomer, this man from another land, was honoured before all of them. They plotted to kill him. How would they do it? Daniel was such a fine fellow, such a good man and scarcely ever seemed to do anything wrong, that they could not pick on him or find fault. It would not be difficult to find some of our faults, would it? There is one thing, they thought. He is very, very religious. He is always praying to his God, the God of the Jews, and if we ask the king to make a decree (a law) that for thirty days nobody is to pray to any god except our king, for we believe our king is a god, we may catch him.

So, the king signed the decree. He did not know what was in their minds. The decree said that anyone who goes *down* on their knees and *prays* to any god except the king within thirty days, will be thrown into the den of lions.

What did Daniel do? Did he *stop* praying? No, of course not. He opened his window looking towards Jerusalem, his loved city, and prayed three times a day: morning, noon and night, the same as ever.

They saw him through the window. "Ah, we've got you." They went to the king; but the king was very fond of Daniel and admired him. He did not know what was really in the minds of those wicked men. What could he do? He had signed the decree and could not change it. It was now the law of the land and even the king had to obey the law of the land. So he had to say, "All right, you will have to put that excellent young man Daniel in amongst the lions." So they did.

But God shut the mouths of the lions. I could well believe, you know, that Daniel went up to them and stroked them. You've seen somebody stroking a lion? I have. God had tamed them and shut their mouths. And in the morning instead of the king seeing a few bones, there was Daniel, alive. "Good morning," he must have said to the king.

When we obey God and are true to Him in front of the whole world and say, "Yes, I love Jesus. I belong to Jesus; I am a Jesus boy or girl and am not ashamed", God will take care of us. Sometimes, people try to do us harm, but God is always watching over us, as He watched over Daniel. Nothing happened to Daniel, because God shut the lions' mouths.

Section Five

Teaching Children About The Church

When children are encouraged to look forward to coming to Church as they do to coming home, they have learned the deepest thing to be known about Christian fellowship.

(a)One Family
(Matthew 23:8)

I wonder if you remember that a few weeks ago I spoke to you about how when we get to heaven, we won't be living in families as we do down here: Daddy, Mummy and the children. Sometimes here there are Granny and Grandpa, Uncle, Aunty, or cousins but there will be not only Grannies and Grandpas but Great-Grannies and Great-great Grannies and Grandpas in heaven. We will all be there together, and it would be very difficult to sort us all out into little families.

I don't know what you thought when I said that, but some of the big people did not like what I said. I am sorry about that, but it is true; that is what it will be like in heaven. We are all going to be one big family of brothers and sisters. I hope YOU wouldn't call your Mummy, 'sister', or call her by her first name; that is not nice for little folk to do, or even big folk. I would never have called my Mother 'Sister' or called her by her name, Helen, even when I was a great, big man and she was an old lady. But up in heaven it will be different because we will all be together in one large family. We will all be brothers and sisters of Jesus.

People down here are called by all sorts of different names: sons, daughters, cousins, aunts, uncles, fathers, mothers, grandmothers, great-grandfathers. People are given titles: sir, lord, duke, doctor, professor, reverend, bishop, priest, pastor, master, Prime Minister or Queen. But in heaven we will all be just plain brothers and sisters of Jesus.

Surely to be a brother or sister of Jesus, God's

Son from heaven, is the most wonderful thing in the world. We would not want to be called anything else. There is no better name, no better title that we could have than that. To be called a lord, or king, or emperor would not be nearly so wonderful as being called brothers and sisters of Jesus. I hope we would want no other name when we go there.

> We are of Thee, the children of Thy love,
> The brothers of Thy well-beloved Son;
> Descend, O Holy Spirit, like a dove,
> Into our hearts, that we may be as one;
> As one with Thee, to whom we ever tend,
> As one with Him, our Brother and our Friend.

(b)One body but all Different
(Ephesians1:4-23)

What kind of world would it be if all of us were exactly the same and looked alike? When you look at a flock of sheep you cannot tell the one from the other unless there is something special about each of them. But Jesus says that the shepherds in His day knew their sheep and gave them names. When I was a boy, the farmers I knew all had names for their cows, their horses, their dogs and their pussy cats.

But what if we were a bit like the sheep - all alike: the same height, and all had the same colour of hair, the same colour of eyes and complexion, the same sort of nose, same face, and same kind of voice? If we all had the same voice we couldn't have choirs: sopranos, altos, tenors and basses, because all the voices would be the same. What if we all walked the same way? What if we all had the same likes? We would not know one another because everybody would be exactly the same. Wouldn't that be strange? We would all be copies of one another and there would be no differences. Like twins? But even twins are different. But there are identical twins that are so alike - and I have known a number of them, so alike that you can't tell the difference and we have to say, "Are you James? Are you John?" or "Are you Mary? Are you Alice?" Although we can't tell, Mummies and Daddies can.

God means us all to be different, because He likes a great mixture. It makes it so rich, when you have people of all ages in the Church. Look around: little boys and girls, big boys and girls, young men and young women, older ones, and very old ones - all together. Some have one colour of hair, some another, and some come from near at hand and some from far away. There are always people from far away here. God loves to stir us all up into a great mixture and make it rich.

But all of us here today - different ages, different work, different homes, different to look at - on the Lord's Day (this is the Lord's Day, Sunday) because we love the Lord Jesus, are all one. He calls all of us to be together. We are a body, not bodies but one body. He wants us to be all different yet one body in Jesus. Isn't that wonderful? There is so much difference in us all, and that is fine, isn't it?

Sometimes we say, "I wouldn't like everyone to be like you" and I wouldn't like everyone to be like me! Sometimes we say, "One of me is enough," or sometimes we say, if we are a little bit angry, "One of you is enough - too many." Yet we are one body in Jesus, and that is wonderful.

One holy Church, one army strong,
One steadfast, high intent.
One working band, one harvest-song,
One King Omnipotent.

(c) Christian Giving
(2 Corinthians 8-9:5)

Have you ever given your Mummy or your Daddy a present? What did you use for money? Where did you get it? You got yours from the Bank? Yes. And you got yours out of your own pocket money. But where did that come from? From Daddy. There is nothing wrong with that because you were not born with money in your hand.

That is exactly like our gifts that we give to God. We are giving Him back what He has given to us. Yes, He has given all to us. He has given us our life. He gave us the world. He made everything. It is all His. God says, "The cattle upon a thousand hills are Mine." The sun, moon and the stars are His. Even Satan is His although God did not make him bad; that was his own wicked self that did that. God made Satan a bright angel but he turned against God. Nevertheless he is still God's. God holds him in His hand and he can only do the bad God allows him to do. Everything in the whole universe is His. Universe means all one - it is all His and He controls it.

He gives us our life, our bodies, our eyes, our ears, our noses for smelling, our lips, our mouths to eat with, our hands to work with, our feet to move. He provides all the money Mummy and Daddy have, whether they have much or little. Everything is from God. He gives us all these things so that we may have a happy life - enjoy our food, have nice clothes and a comfortable house to live in. He gives us all those good things because He loves us. *But He wants us to give a share of it back to Him.*

Why does He want us to give a share of it back to Him when He has got so much? You might say, "Oh God, You have got plenty; You don't need my pennies." Why does He want our pennies? It shows that we love Him, and then, as one of you said, we share by giving to other children. But you are giving it back to God by giving it to others. I think that's great!

We give Thee but Thine own.
Whate'er the gift may be,
All that we have is Thine alone,
A trust, O Lord, from Thee.

(d)Evangelism
(Matthew 4:12-22)

We read this morning about Jesus walking along the shores of the Lake of Galilee and finding four men there who were preparing to go fishing. Jesus said to each of them, "Come and follow Me." And they left their nets, and their boats, and followed Jesus. And He said, "I will make you fish for men" - not for fish but for men. What did Jesus mean? What did He mean when He said He would make them fishers of men? Well, you know how these men were fishing in the Lake, don't you? They had their nets and their boats, and as the nets dropped into the water, the fish would swim into them and be caught.

Now, there are different kinds of fishing nets. There is the TRAWL net, which is a great bag of a net, cast out of the trawler. The boat is called a trawler because it trails this bag of a net, with its great, open mouth, catching fish, including those that lie on the bottom, the flat fish.

There is the DRIFT net. Boats that use that are called DRIFTERS. Big boats they were. My grandfather, and I think six of my uncles had them. One was called *The Jasper* after the precious stone in the book of the Revelation. Some of my uncles later had a boat they called *The Golden West* because their name was West, and I suppose the money they made, catching herring, was golden. There were golden coins - sovereigns in those days. The drifter let out its nets with corks at the top and weights at the bottom so that the net hung in the sea like a great curtain of net, like a wall. It caught all the fish for they swam into the net. The size of the mesh is the size that lets in herring but won't let them right through because the gills are caught. The fish is caught; it can neither go forward nor backward. Poor fish - caught.

The SEINE net is let out of the boat. If it is salmon fishing they are engaged in, it will be a cobble boat. It spends out its net from the boat, the boat makes a big circle, then draws in the circle of the net till it catches the fish. You can see fishermen doing this for salmon down at the river Dee. They used to have a little hut there. The boat has the net heaped up at the stern of the boat, and as it moves out to the centre of the river the net pays out and the boat turns back to the shore in a wide circle. They then haul in the net. I have stood for ages watching them to see if the net had anything in it. Salmon are lovely, silver fish.

Of course, boys and girls, you can catch fish yourselves. You can get a net like a little cup on the end of a cane. We used to call these BANDIE CATCHERS, because the little fish we named 'bandies'. There is HOOK and LINE fishing. Have you done that with a rod and line? Boys sometimes sit on the pier at the harbour with only a line and a hook on the end of it with a worm. They cast it into the sea. The nasty little nick in the hook catches the fish and it cannot escape.

There are other ways of catching fish. Sometimes boats go out to sea with lines with many hooks on them. They catch lots of fish that way. My mother used to bait these many hooks when she was a girl, for her father and her brothers to go what they called LINE FISHING.

You can catch lobsters and crabs with CAGES left on the sea bottom with perhaps a cod-head in them for bait to catch them.

All these methods are used to catch fish of one kind or another. But Jesus said to His disciples, "I will make you fishers of MEN." Men have to be caught for Jesus. Boys and girls have to be caught. Just as fish don't want to be caught, cut up and eaten, neither do boys and girls want to be caught for Jesus, because they don't know how good He is. He does not eat them up, but He blesses them in every way. He loves them and at last takes them to heaven to be with Himself, and His Father, and the Holy Spirit.

Men and women and boys and girls have to be caught for Jesus. We have to try to attract them to Jesus Christ and tell them how good Jesus is. We have to use nets, and hooks, and baits to do that. How do we do it? We have to let Jesus' Spirit shine out of our faces. We have to learn to smile as Jesus smiled on people to show them how good He is. We have to speak loving words, and sympathetic words when people are sad. We attract people to Jesus because they see how happy and well Jesus has made us. Some people are not good hooks to catch people for Jesus, because they look glum, and sour, or are surly in their speech and selfish in their behaviour, and push and shove in a crowd as if to say, " ME first". A Jesus person would say if someone was pushing, "YOU first", and would smile.

I shop around the corner there on Saturday morning and when I go into any shop I say to myself, "William, SHINE for Jesus." Smile as Jesus would smile and be ready to speak nicely to anyone beside you. If anyone bumps into you, be nice to them. Or, you may hold the door open for someone. When I go to hospital to see sick people, I say to myself when I walk down a hospital ward with beds on either side with sick people in them, that I must look interested and kindly, and perhaps smile and say something to this one, or that one in bed, whom I may not know. Then I come to the one I came to visit and I speak kindly to him, show the love of Jesus and just do what Jesus would do if He was in that ward.

You, boys and girls, have to be Jesus at school, and at play. That's the way to be fishers of other boys and girls for Jesus.

May I ask you this question: Have you ever told a friend, your neighbour, or someone you play with about Jesus? Or have you ever brought a friend to Jesus? Have you ever brought anyone to Church or Sunday School to hear about Jesus, to worship with Jesus' people here? That is what Jesus is saying to His disciples, "I want to make you fishers of men." And you know He is saying the same to you.

Help me the slow of heart to move
By some clear winning word of love;
Teach me the wayward feet to stay,
And guide them in the homeward way.

Section Six

Teaching Children To Grow As Believers

The faith of children nurtured in the Word of God may be so simple that nothing disturbs it, but as they grow and their knowledge increases, they need to be fortified by ever greater and deeper understanding of the power of God's Word and Spirit to keep them and make them grow.

(a) Loving one another
(Genesis 30:1-24)

We were reading in the Bible this morning about two sisters who were jealous of one another. They didn't like one another very much. That was very sad. I want to speak to you about that for a little .

Jesus said we are to love one another. We are to love one another because we are all made by God to be His children. *How can you love someone you don't like?* It is not easy, is it? If you really don't like a person it is not very easy to love them. Yet, Jesus said, we are to love one another. He loves all that He has made: the animals, the flowers, the trees, the rivers and the seas, and boys and girls, and men and women. He loves them all. He made them, to give Him pleasure. He loves even the worst. He loved even Judas. It was Judas who got Jesus killed, yet Jesus called him *Friend*.

I don't think that Jesus would have liked Judas very much because He knew that he was going to get Him killed. Yet, He loved him and called him His friend. How could He love him and try to save him even at the end? How could He love someone that even He did not like very much? The answer to that is because His heart is absolutely full of love, even for Judas, whom He knew was going to get Him killed. Isn't that wonderful?

Jesus is the one who can help us to learn to love those we don't like, because He did it. His Spirit is within us when we believe in Him and receive Him. The Lord Jesus is in your heart, isn't He? Say, Yes. It's true, isn't it? He can help you to love those that you don't like.

(b)Loving till it hurts
(1John 3:16-18)

I want to ask you a special question. It may seem to you a silly question but I am going to ask it. *Do you love your Mummy?*

That's good. But, how much? And why? Why do you love your Mummy? Come on now, you philosophers. When you love your Mummy because of what she gives you and what she does for you and all that, you know what that is called? Well, you know where food is kept? In a cupboard, a fridge, or a pantry. This kind of love is called *Cupboard love,* because she cooks nice things for you, gives you nice things to wear, and looks after you when you are sick.

But there is another kind of love. God's love is not *Cupboard love.* God loves us when we have nothing to give Him but our nasty, nasty sins. That is all we have to give to God. We are naughty, naughty children, aren't we? But He loves us, although we have nothing to give Him at all. He loved us so much, little children and big children, that He sent His Son to die for us. That is a different kind of love, isn't it? That is love that loves till it hurts! It is real love. That is Jesus' love. He loves and loves even when people have nothing to give to Him at all but their nastiness.

Do you love your Mummy until it hurts you? What do I mean? Well, Mummy may say, "Little boy, little girl, I want you to do this for me, do this little job, run this little errand. I want you to be quiet because baby will be disturbed." But you are playing and having fun, enjoying yourself and you don't listen, you disobey, you ignore your Mummy. You don't love her until it hurts you, because you would stop pleasing yourself and please her if you did. You would stop doing what was wrong and would do what was right even if you did not like to do it. So, to love your Mummy as she loves you, and God and Jesus love you, is to love even when it hurts, when you have to do things you don't like.

Do you love her like that? Do you do things for her you don't like and don't want to do? That's Jesus' love because He loved us even when it hurt Him, even to come and die for us. Mummies (and don't forget Daddies) are listening to what I have said. I hope you are too.

(c)Jacob humbled
(2 Corinthians 12:7)

I wonder what you know about Jacob. He was a twin; his brother's name was Esau. God told their mother He was going to bless Jacob more than He was going to bless Esau. He had chosen Jacob before he was born, to bless him. She, of course, remembered a thing like that because God had told her. I think she told Jacob. At any rate Jacob became very proud. He even stole from his brother Esau because he thought he was God's special child and could do what he liked. He *was* God's special child, but that did not mean he could do what he liked. Jacob had to run away from home and go far away into another land, for his brother would have killed him if he had got a hold of him.

After living for twenty years in that country, God said to Jacob, "Go back, Jacob, go back home." "Oh," said Jacob, "what about Esau?" But he had to go. On his way back he gathered great flocks and herds, cows and sheep. People then did not have much money but they had animals instead.

He had lots of flocks and herds to appease Esau. To APPEASE somebody is to try to end their anger so that they will not be angry with you any longer. Jacob reached near to where Esau was coming to meet him. He thought Esau might be coming with men to kill them all, so he spent the night praying. But it was a funny kind of praying because he was arguing with God all the time, as if he knew better than God. God got tired of all this arguing. They argued together until it was morning and the sun rose. Then God said, "I have had enough of this." Jacob of course was arguing because he was proud, because he was a special child and he thought he could say things to God that other people could not say. God was grieved with him. What do you think God did to Jacob to stop him arguing and being such a proud man? He thumped him hard and broke his thigh. That's right. It could not be mended. (There weren't pins in those days. Some people in this congregation have had their thighs mended.) So Jacob had a cripple leg until he died.

Was it cruel of God to do this to Jacob? No, it was not. God wanted to bless Jacob but He could not until he was humble, until his pride was taken away. The only way God could bless Jacob was by humbling him and making him walk with a limp. After He had broken his thigh and Jacob was a cripple for life God said, "Now, I am going to give you a new name." I hope you know his new name. It is very important to know his new name. Jacob was the father of twelve sons - does that tell you something? Think ! 'Israel' was Jacob's new name.

Isn't that a wonderful story? It is a sore one because Jacob was so proud that God was going to bless him, that God had to humble him and give him what Paul calls, "a thorn in the flesh." We are going to sing a hymn about Jacob at Peniel, the place where this happened to him.

Come, O Thou Traveller unknown,
Whom still I hold but cannot see;
My company before is gone,
And I am left alone with Thee;
With Thee all night I mean to stay,
And wrestle till the break of day.

(d)Not Eye-pleasers
(Colossians 3:22 - 4:1)

I am going to tell you a story about long ago when I was a boy going to school. I am thinking about a time when I was a little bit older than any of you. Sometimes the teacher left the room to go to the headmaster's office. She would say, "Now, I have given you work to do and you will continue doing your writing while I am away just the same as if I were sitting at my table. You will continue working and you will behave while I am out and until I come back." But as soon as the door was closed we began to talk, and more than talk - to get out of our seats. That was a very daring thing to do unless the teacher called you. We began throwing paper pellets about. Then, thinking the teacher might be out for quite a time all sorts of things took place in the classroom.

Suddenly, the door opened, and the teacher was there standing in the doorway. Everyone ran to his seat and put his head down as if he was doing his work. But it was too late because she had seen us. She came to her table and rapped the table and said, "Look up and listen to me." And she gave us a lecture. She told us what naughty boys and girls we were and that it was wrong to do what we had been doing because we should be doing our work whether she was watching or not. She used words that are found in the Bible, "'You are not to be eye-pleasers.' You are to do what is right and do your work whether the teacher is watching you, whether she is in the room with you or not. You are there to learn, and you must learn all the time; that is what you are in school to do. There is a playground outside for having fun - and there is a time for that. But in the classroom you are here to work."

The Bible speaks about people who are eye-pleasers, who are only going to please their master while the master is there and looking. God's Word says that Christians should not do that because they are working not only for their earthly master, but for the Lord Jesus. If you are Christians and you are in school you are not only working for your teacher, but, out of love, you are working for Jesus. If you are a Christian you do everything for the Lord Jesus because He saved you from your sins by His blood. So, if you serve Him, you serve Him well whether anybody else is looking - the teacher, or the master- or not.

You see, God never leaves the room. He is always there and He is always watching. He is not watching, like a teacher or a master, to pounce on you if you do something wrong, but He is watching. He sees all that happens, even in the darkest night. He sees and He knows, not only what we do and what we say, but He knows what we think! We must not think what is wrong because He sees that, too. He is never absent, never leaves the room, never falls asleep. He is always watching twenty-four hours a day. So if we love the Lord Jesus and want to serve Him then we must remember that He is watching us. We will want to do for Him the very best that we can do.

God is always near me,
Hearing what I say,
Knowing all my thoughts and deeds,
All my work and play.

God is always near me;
In the darkest night
He can see me just the same
As by mid-day light.

God is always near me
Though so young and small;
Not a look or word or thought,
But God knows it all.

(e) Shining for Jesus
(Matthew 5:14-16)

I was once at a wedding in Lanark in the south of Scotland. When I drove back, it was dark. It was also a rather dirty night, with snow and sleet. The roads were dirty and some of those great lorries were splashing up lumps of snow and mud. Because my car is very light in colour, it soon shows all the dirt. "It must be getting quite a mess," I thought. As I went on through the night, the lights of the car grew dimmer, and dimmer, and dimmer. I kept saying to myself, "These lights are very poor to-night, that is not the brightness they usually have. There must be something wrong with them." I drew into a lay-by and got out to look at them.

What was wrong? Can you guess? Yes, it was snow and mud sticking to the glass. You could not see the lights for dirt. No wonder they were not shining brightly. I cleaned them and then they shone brightly, the brightest lights on the road, I think!

The lesson this teaches us, boys and girls, is that we are to shine for Jesus but to do this we must be clean. Jesus said, "I am the light of the world." If you have Jesus in your heart, then you are to be a light in the world. Jesus is in your heart, but when your heart gets dirty, people won't see His light shining from you. We frown sometimes when we sulk, and we look such unhappy, miserable and naughty little children that nobody can see Jesus' light shining through us at all. It is all dimmed. But then we cry to Jesus, "Lord Jesus, are You there? Please help me not to be a sulky child, or a naughty child. Help me not to frown, because I have to shine

Your light out of my face." For when our faces and our hearts are all covered over with the dirt of sin, we have to be cleaned so that the light can shine out again.

Then people will see it and say, "Ah, what a nice little boy. What a lovely little girl! She must have Jesus in her heart for He is shining and making her smile and be nice, and kind, and happy and good. That little boy never says bad words." Do you remember the word I told you was bad for little boys and girls to say to Mummy or Daddy, or even your teacher when you go to school? It was "NO." "No" is a bad word. Don't say, "No, I won't." To shine for Jesus means that we will say, "Yes Mummy, I will go; Yes Daddy, I will do it at once." That is Jesus' light shining out of our hearts.

"Jesus bids us shine, first of all for Him
Well He sees and knows it, if our light grows dim.
He looks down from heaven to see us shine,
You in your small corner and I in mine."

(f) Making Your Wedding Garment
(Matthew 22:10-14)

In the reading about a wedding feast we heard about clothes that people wear for weddings. The Bible says that when we get to heaven we are going to wear very special wedding clothes. We are all going to have a white robe. The white robe we are to wear in heaven is really a gift from Jesus. It stands for our salvation. The Bible says it is "the robe of Christ's righteousness", and all those who are saved by Jesus' blood will have these white robes, washed in Jesus' blood. Isn't that strange? Robes, washed in Jesus' blood but they are white, bright, shining and beautiful.

But the Bible also says a very difficult thing that you might not understand. I'm sure the grown-ups don't understand it either, and I certainly don't. The Bible says that we make our wedding robe for heaven. It can't be true, can it, that the wedding robe we wear in heaven is Jesus' robe, which He gives to us, while it yet says in Revelation 19:8 that the Lord's bride, that is, His church, all who believe and love Jesus, "has made herself ready," and she is going to be wearing "fine linen, bright and clean"?

John explains what he means: he says, fine linen stands for "the righteous acts of the saints." He says that the wedding robe we wear is something that we make ourselves, by our good deeds, the things we do because we love Jesus. We can give somebody a cup of cold water or care for people or help them in another way. These are good deeds done for Jesus' sake.

Which would be the truth? The Bible says the

robes we will wear in heaven will be Jesus' robes, but it also says that we are making them by our good deeds. They can't both be true, can they? Either the robe we wear in heaven, at the wedding of Jesus Christ, the Bridegroom, to His Church is given, or it is made. They can't both be true, can they? Oh, it is certainly Jesus' robe that we shall wear. Listen to the wonderful words of Isaiah,"I delight greatly in the Lord, my soul rejoices in my God for He has clothed me with garments of salvation and arrayed me in a robe of righteousness, as a bridegroom adorns his head like a priest and a bride adorns herself with jewels." So it is certainly Jesus' robe. Yet, John says here that the robe we wear is a robe that is made of our good deeds that we do for Jesus' sake in this world. They are both true.

This is how I like to think of it: the robe we receive is Jesus' robe, washed in His blood. But if we just scrape into heaven "by the skin of our teeth," because we haven't done many good deeds, or if we have just believed in Jesus but we have not loved Him enough to do many good things, I think we may be wearing a very plain white robe. But if we not only believe in Jesus and are saved by His precious blood, but we so much love Him that we want to tell people about Jesus and be kind to them, then I think that we will not be wearing a plain white robe but one that will be - how would you put it, girls? - "Embroidered" would you say? Some brides make their own wedding dresses. If you saw some of the royal wedding dresses they are embroidered with pearls, jewels, sequins and all sorts of embroidered flowers, and are very, very beautiful.

I believe this is how we should think of our wedding garments: we have been given Jesus' robe of righteousness and He is saying to us, "Now, by doing many, many good deeds for Me, embroider that robe, and make it look very beautiful." Then those who have done most for Jesus will look the most beautiful.

Do you think that is right?

Teaching Children About Heaven

Ah, this will appeal to children because they have such wonderful imaginations that they find it much easier to believe in heaven than many grown-ups.

(a)People Dying and Going to Heaven
(Isaiah 35)

When you are young and small, it is nice to be growing up and learning more. But keep growing, and growing and you will learn more and more. You will move from school to work. Then you may work many, many years with all sorts of wonderful things happening to you throughout your lives until you grow old. But people can grow sick and die long before they are very old. We say it is so sad when some that we have loved very much and known for many years die and we lose them. We miss them, and we say, "Oh, why have people to become sick? Why have people to become so old that they are not able to come to Church? Why, when we have known them so long and loved them so much must they die and go away?" We put them in a box in the ground and we see them no more. We are sore and we weep because we miss them so much.

But there is another side to that, because, for those who love the Lord Jesus, death is only the death of their bodies. You already know this, but I am telling you again. The soul, the real part inside, does not die. God has made it immortal. Our souls cannot die. When our body dies and is laid in the ground, the soul goes marching on. Our loved ones, those that we miss so much, are not dead. Their bodies may be crumbling away but they are not dead. They are alive and well, and happy with Jesus. We need to remember that. They have gone to a land of beauty and flowers where no one ever grows old, no one is ever sick, and no one is ever unhappy, and of course no one ever dies. No tears there!

It is natural for us, when we lose our loved ones, to shed tears because we love them so much and miss them. But there will be no tears up there. God will wipe all the tears right out of their eyes. There will be no tears, no unhappiness. We are going to live in a world with Jesus where nothing ever goes wrong. Everything will be perfect. We will never grow old, never be separated from our loved ones, never be separated from Jesus. There will be nothing to cry about, nothing wrong, at all, at all, at all.

When we weep and are sad about our loved ones that we have lost, we must also remember this and be glad for them. If we could phone up to them and say, "Aren't you coming back to see us?" they would say, "Oh no, if you could see what a beautiful place I am in, you would want to come too. No, I can't come down there. I want to stay here because it is so wonderful." That is what they would say. Isn't that great?

Christ our Lord is ever near
Those who follow Him;
But we cannot see Him here,
For our eyes are dim;
There is a most happy place,
Where men always see His face.

(b)Glorification
(Revelation1:17-18)

"What is this I have today?"

"A torch."

"And this?"

"A microphone."

Now, what is the difference between the one and the other? This wire on the microphone goes here and that one there. But there are no wires on the torch. Mr. Ross, our organist has a light there. Look at his, and look at mine. His light has got wires and is plugged in, like the microphone. But my torch is not plugged in; all the power comes from inside it. I put batteries in and the electricity is inside.

Wouldn't it be fun if our bodies were all wired up to heaven and Jesus! Yes, but there is no need for that because Jesus has put a battery, His Spirit, in us. It should be charging all the time so that we grow brighter and brighter.

Now we don't have a torch light on all the time. Once or twice I've popped my torch into the cubby hole in my car, with the light still on. Then the battery goes done and the light goes out. We switch on the light when it is dark and we want to see in to some corner. It is like that with the battery Spirit Jesus has put within those who love Him. The battery Spirit is only within people who love Jesus. There are lots of people who do not love Jesus but the Spirit is not in them. If we really love Jesus, then we love Him because He has put His battery Spirit within us. But He has not switched us on yet. One day we are going to shine.

Once Jesus went up a mountain with His disciples, Peter, and James, and John. Do you know what His Father in heaven did? He switched Him on and He grew bright and shining and shone like the sun. His clothes were gleaming white. But it was just for a little time.

When Jesus went back to heaven, the Father switched Jesus on permanently. This is what John saw in his vision that we read about in the book of Revelation. John saw how bright He was. Saul too on the Damascus road, at mid-day, when the sun was shining its brightest, saw Jesus brighter than the sun. Jesus shone out and said, "Saul, Saul, why are you hurting Me?"

When we get to heaven, the Father is going to switch us on too, and we are going to shine. All our batteries will be working and we are going to shine, and shine, and shine in glory. Isn't that wonderful?

But now, remember what I said earlier: if we really love the Lord Jesus and pray to Him and obey Him, and do what is good - never say "No" to Mummy, or do nasty things to our friends - then that is because His battery Spirit is within us. Then we can look forward to the day when God is going to switch us on, and we will shine, and shine, and SHINE!

(c)A Heavenly Prize-giving
(Mark 9:38-41)

The world is full of people, and the number is always increasing. If it grows much bigger we will have hardly any room; we will all have to stand close together, there will be so many people in the world. There are lots of very bad people in the world, but there are also many good people, Jesus people. God has allowed the good people and the bad people to be together in the world, and they all seem to be mixed up. But He is watching. He knows the Jesus people, the good people and He knows the bad people. One day, at the end of the world, Jesus is going to gather everybody together and He is going to separate the good from the bad. He calls them the sheep and the goats. He is going to put the bad to His left and the good to His right hand. Then He is going to give prizes. There is going to be a prizegiving. Anyone who has given someone else, who was perhaps very thirsty in a hot land, a cup of cold water because they loved Jesus and loved people, will get a prize. He will get a prize for being kind to someone and saying, "Look, Jesus loves you and I love you and I see you are very thirsty, have a cup of this nice, cold water."

There are to be prizes then for those who are good to thirsty people, and for those who are good to hungry people, and for those who are good to people who are strangers, foreigners, people who have come a long distance from another land and are feeling lost. You might say, "Come and have lunch with us" or "Come and have tea with us." Those who do that because Jesus would do it are going to get a prize. If they give clothes to people who are naked, especially who are shivering in the cold, they will get a prize. Those who are kind to the sick - Christian doctors and nurses and others who love Jesus and who know that Jesus would have done that - they are going to get a prize. Those who go to see people in prison (you know some good people can be in prison; John the Baptist went to prison and some people are in prison just because they love Jesus) or send gifts to people in prison will also be rewarded. All those who do these things are going to get a prize.

Jesus says that when He has His prize-giving in heaven He will say to His people, "You are going to get a prize for looking after the hungry," and "You are going to get a prize for looking after the thirsty," and "You are going to get a prize for looking after the strangers who came into your town," and "You are going to get a prize for looking after the naked". Jesus will put it like this, "You are going to get a prize for giving Me a cup of cold water, and for feeding Me with nice food and taking Me into your house. You are going to get a prize for giving Me clothes and for looking after Me when I was sick and when I was in prison." They will reply: "But Lord, we never did that to You."

He will say, "Yes you did, when you did it to those that I love that were hungry, and naked, and thirsty, and lonely, and strangers, and in prison, and very sick. You did it to Me."

It is like Christmas time when we give gifts to poorer people. We gather our Christmas gifts and they are taken to the poorest children in the town because we can't send our gifts up to heaven. Even if we did, Jesus would say, "Send these birthday gifts of Mine down to these poor children I have in Aberdeen, who don't have any toys and any nice things." It is a bit like that. When we are doing kind things to people because we love Jesus (and that must be the reason. Some people do kind things but not for Jesus' sake ; they hate Jesus), then we are going to get a prize when we go upstairs to heaven. Jesus is going to say, "You did it to Me because you did it with the love that I have for people in My heart." Isn't that lovely?

"Inasmuch as you did it to one of the least of these My brothers, you did it to Me."

Section Eight

Teaching
Children
How
God
Helps
Them

Teaching Children How God Helps Them

The Bible is full of help about how to draw on the divine resources to live the good life and serve the Lord. Why should little children who are learning to love the Lord not be taught within their understanding how to draw upon these resources?

(a)Jesus - Our Advocate
(1 John 2 :1-2)

Sometimes you hear stories, as you will do when you go later on to Primary School. Once you can read, you can read stories, and nowadays we can see stories on television. I saw a story on television the other day - I wonder if any of you saw it. It was the story of a boy, a bit bigger than any of you, who stole radio sets from a shop. He hid them in his garden shed. One day, coming home from school he saw the police car at his door, and he shook, and he shook, and he shook, and then crept in. There was the policeman speaking to his Daddy. The policeman had found out that he had stolen these radio sets.

Later on he was taken to court before a judge. The judge was a lady but she was quite stern and Tony - that was the boy's name - was very frightened. The judge said, "Stand up Tony, tell us why you did this." He could not say very much because he knew he had done wrong. When he was finished, he was asked to sit down. The judge then spoke to two people behind Tony in the court. Can you imagine who they would be?

"His Mummy and his Daddy."

That is absolutely right: his Mummy and his Daddy. The judge said, first to Mummy, "Have you anything to say?" She spoke about her boy. Then Daddy: had he anything to say? And he spoke about his boy. Tony was put on probation, that is to say he was to be watched for a whole year, to see that he did not do anything wrong again. But if his Mummy and Daddy had not been there to speak for him and say the very best they could about him, he might have been sent to a Young Person's prison. Tony had two advocates: his Mummy and his Daddy. Of course when big people do wrong they are taken to the big court where they have an advocate, someone who is trained, who comes and speaks for them and says the very best he can for them. So big people have advocates too.

All who love Jesus have an advocate. Do you love Jesus? Then you have an advocate, who is Jesus Himself. I will tell you what He does. If you are naughty - and you are naughty sometimes - your Mummy will ask you, before you go to sleep, "Are you sorry?" I don't think you would sleep well if you were not! If you tell Jesus that you are sorry, He will turn to His Father in heaven and say, "Forgive him. Take him back into Your heart because I died and shed My blood to forgive his sins."

When we do wrong, and then say to Jesus that we are sorry, He speaks to the Father who replies, "All right, you are forgiven; but don't do it again. I take you back into My arms and I will love you." That is because of Jesus Christ, our advocate.

(b) The Indwelling Holy Spirit
2 Timothy 1:12-18

If I were to ask you if you loved Jesus, you would all say, "Yes," wouldn't you? I hope you would really mean it, that you really loved Jesus for what He has done for us on the Cross by the shedding of His blood. We ought to be grateful to Him for dying for us. If you really love Jesus it means He is in your heart. You could not love Jesus unless He was in your heart. Many people don't love Jesus, they hate Him. If you love Him, He is in your heart.

Do you know what it means to have Jesus in your heart? God is three Persons - only one God: the Father, the Son, (Jesus Christ who came to earth), and the Holy Spirit (more difficult to think of Him but it is the Holy Spirit who brings Jesus Christ to dwell in our hearts). Jesus came down to save us and then went back to heaven to send down His own Spirit into the hearts of those who love Him.

If Jesus' Spirit is in your heart, (and I am saying you can't love Jesus if He is not) think what has happened? God who made all things - the sun, the moon and the stars; who controls the thunder, the lightning, the rain; who makes the sun shine, has planted His own Spirit, the Spirit of Jesus, in your heart to assure you that you are His forever. He will never leave you and He will never let you go. Even when you die He will be with you and keep you. That is *tremendous*, that God has put Himself, through Jesus, by the Spirit in your little heart. That is *tremendous*!

It is a bit like this: you know your Mummy and your Daddy put money in the bank. They don't keep it at home because a robber might come and steal it. They say to the banker, "Please keep that money for me. It's mine but I want you to keep it for me." Just like that God is saying to you, "Look, I'm putting my money (that is Jesus by His Spirit) into you, and you are My bank. You have to keep Jesus' Spirit in you and look after Him and be good to Him."

But then you might say, "How can little folk like us keep the great Spirit of God in our tiny, little hearts?"

Well, although He has "deposited" Jesus in the bank of your heart, He is saying to you, "Now, you can't keep Him properly there, you can't be as kind and nice to Him as you ought to be unless you have My help."

We have to ask God's help so that we keep Jesus happy in our hearts. We won't be able to unless we ask God's help to do that. We must say, "Lord, You have put Your great Spirit that made the world in my heart; You must help me to keep and guard Your Spirit, to guard Your Jesus and be good to Him and kind to Him."

If you ask God to do that, He will. We will grow up to be as strong Christians as our Mummies and Daddies. Some Mummies and Daddies have little time for God, or the Church, or Sunday. You meet their children at school, who never go to Church or Sunday School. Aren't you glad that your Mummies and Daddies, who love Jesus Christ, are strong Christians who say, " You can speak to Jesus every day of the week. But you must come with us and worship God especially on Sunday?" Aren't you glad?

(c)Guardian Angels
(1 John 4 :13-21)

Anybody here who has never been afraid? Graeme is afraid of the ghost train.   Are some of you afraid of creepy crawlies? Some of the girls might be afraid of mice,dogs, cows, horses, traffic, thunder, things that go bump in the night, or squeak, or scream? Are you afraid of nightmares, when you wake in the night and have had a bad dream and someone is coming to get you?

"No."

Oh, brave girl! Stories about hobgoblins and foul fiends? Are you afraid of the dark?

"No."

You are afraid of nothing? You are a wonderful chap. But others are afraid of the dark. I want to speak to you about being afraid in the dark. The dark,when Mummy puts out the light, is really just the same but with the light out. It cannot hurt you. There is nothing in the dark to hurt you, and if Mummy put on the light, you would see everything is the same. But we fear the nasty creatures, bogey men, might come and get us. But nothing changes. God will not run away from us. He sees in the dark. The psalmist tells us God sees in the dark just as much as He sees in the light.

Something else: our guardian angel will never run away when we are afraid. He will come nearer us then than when it is light. Did you know you had a guardian angel? It tells us in the Bible that every little child, every baby has a guardian angel. I think every child has one all to themselves. Now your guardian angel is different from yours, and yours.

We have all got a guardian angel to look after us.
so we have absolutely nothing to fear.

The best way to take away our fear is to love
Jesus. When you love Jesus, you pray to Jesus and
He takes away your fear. His guardian angel comes
close and takes your fear away.

We have to grow up, boys and girls, not being
afraid of the dark or of horrid things, because
Jesus' guardian angel is with us, and he will look
after us, and keep us, and bless us.

In heavenly love abiding,
No change my heart shall fear;
And safe is such confiding,
For nothing changes here:
The storm may roar without me,
My heart may low be laid;
But God is round about me,
And can I be dismayed?

Wherever He may guide me,
No want shall turn me back;
My Shepherd is beside me,
And nothing can I lack.
His wisdom ever waketh,
His sight is never dim;
He knows the way He taketh,
And I will walk with Him.

(d) God's People are Precious to Him
(Zechariah 2:8)

Boys and girls of all ages, I want you to turn up a text. It is nearly at the end of the Old Testament, the second last book, Zechariah 2:8, only a little part of the verse. I will tell you what it is about. God is speaking to His people, who because of their sins had been captives in Babylon for seventy years until they had learned to be true to their own God, Jehovah.

At the end of the seventy years, God says to them, "Run back to Jerusalem and build the city again." He tells them how much He cares for them, how He will never let them go. He had sent them into captivity to punish them for their sins. But now they are coming back like someone who has been sent out of the classroom if he has been naughty, or out of the room at home, and teacher or Mummy would come and say, "All right, you can come in now. You are forgiven." This is what God is saying to His people. He is telling them how much He loves them.

Half way through verse eight He says, "He who touches you (all Christians of course) touches the apple of My eye." What is the apple of your eye? It means the pupil of your eye. Look into someone else's eye. It is the little dark, round spot in the centre of the eyeball. That is the "apple" of your eye. The whole eye is very, very sensitive: it is easily hurt and needs to be protected very, very carefully because if we lose or damage our eye, we may not see. Look again at your friends' eyes and see how wonderfully God has protected our eyes from harm, or hurt, or injury. First of all He has encased it in a wonderful sheath, all the flesh and skin round about. Then He has given our eyes, lids to close, to protect them from wind and cold and grit that would get into our eyes and hurt and injure them. Then He has given them windscreen washers and wipers. Tears are the washers, and lashes are the wipers that wipe away the things that would damage and prevent us from seeing properly. And He has given them eyebrows to stand guard over our eyes.

So, God is really saying to His people - and that includes us if we love the Lord Jesus and believe in Him - that we are like the pupils of His eyes to Him, that He guards against His enemies. That is very wonderful. He will guard us as anyone would guard his eyes. Sometimes you see people wearing dark glasses or a shade to protect their eyes from the sun, or the wind, or from dust. He says He will protect us, and guard us, and care for us, as He does the pupil of His own eye.

But there is more to it than that, boys and girls. This word "apple" in the original language of the Bible means something more than apple. It means "the little man in the eye". What can that mean? Well, you turn again and look in your friend's eye. What can you see? Their eye is like a little mirror. Who do you see there? You see *yourself.* You have two pictures of yourself; one in each eye, as you look in. When you look into people's eyes you don't see *them* (you have to look deeper for that) but you can see yourself. If you move away from the other person's eyes, the picture is gone. But that is exactly what God is saying. He has got not only a picture of us in His eye - that would fade if we went away - but He has got us in His eye, keeping us, watching us, guarding us all the time. The apostle Paul says that he had the Philippians, whom he loved very much, in his heart. That is what God means here by using this figure about the apple (the pupil) of the eye and the little man in the eye. He says, "Oh, I have got you here."

Sometimes people, when their loved ones are far away from them, may have a special picture of them quite prominent in the house, so that they see them every time they pass. When you look at the picture you think of them and look forward to seeing them again. But when they are with you, you don't need the picture to remind you of them. It is just like that with God. He has us in His eyes. We are the little man in His eye and He is watching over us. If we believe in Him, trust Him and love Him, He will never, never let us go, and will protect us far, far more than all those wonderful things around the eye: the lid, the lashes and the tears. He will protect us from harm.

> God will never leave thee;
> All thy wants He knows,
> Feels the pains that grieve thee,
> Sees thy cares and woes.

(e)Worry
(Matthew 6:25-34)

I want to talk to you about worrying. The part we read in the Bible was all about worrying - about what we were to eat and drink, and so on. The Bible says that your life is more important than your food and your drink. You are more important than what you wear. Birds don't worry - at least we don't think they do - although they sure fight. They have been fighting in my garden over the berries in the cotoneaster bushes all the week, and I think some of them must be sick. They certainly don't sow grain like farmers, so they don't reap it or store it into barns, even as squirrels store nuts. They pick up grains of corn or wheat where they fall, or berries in the bushes. They find water somewhere. That is how they live, so they don't need to worry.

We could not all go to the fields and pick grain. Jesus' disciples did one day because they were hungry, but we couldn't all go out and do that. We do pick wild berries. We couldn't all go out and scoop up water from the burns - it would not be clean enough for one thing. But we do have reservoirs to give us lots of pure, clean water. We can't do what the birds do.

But Jesus tells us not to worry about these things because worry kills people. It makes their minds and bodies sick. Children as well as big folk worry. What do you worry about? What keeps you from sleeping at night? Someone under the bed, or you have dreamed of something and you wake and worry? You don't worry about food, do you? It's Mummy who worries about food. I think we should say sometimes, "Oh Mummy, don't worry about food so much, what we are going to have for the next meal, it will be all right." Sometimes Mummies worry: "What are we going to have for dinner tomorrow? Will the children like it?"

Then there is what we wear. Birds have lovely feather coats. Sheep have wool, foxes and pussy cats have fur. Flowers have lovely clothes. The Bible speaks about flowers being clothes with lovely colours and lovely forms. They don't need to put on clothes because they look beautiful as they are. We might not look beautiful if we hadn't any clothes on. But we need clothes also to keep us warm.

Little people as much as big people think a lot about clothes. Girls think about their nice dresses and the proper shoes to go with them. Even boys think about their trousers, football boots and so on. Jesus says we think too much about this. Someone has said that the best thing to do about clothes is to put them on and forget about them. But people don't want to forget about them. They want people to see them: "Were you noticing my new dress? Anybody noticing my new coat - my new shoes?" We are taking too much thought about what we wear. We are to wear our clothes to keep ourselves warm and to cover ourselves up, not to show them off. If you are worrying, or thinking about that all the time, you are not thinking about important things.

We must think, just as Mummies must think, of food. We must think about what we will buy when we need a new coat. But we must not worry about them. Worry is thinking when you don't need to be thinking. It is very nice, as someone has said, sometimes just to stand and stare. We are all so busy in cities that we haven't time to stand and stare, or let our minds run down.

Worry is thinking when you don't need to be thinking or when you should be thinking of other things. Some of you are at school and some are just going to school and you will be worried about that, and the teacher, and reading and sums. Jesus says, "Don't worry. It is all right to plan, but don't worry." He tells little children not to worry, and if you learn as little children, not to worry, when you grow up you'll look nice and young, even when you are seventy and eighty. Your Mummies and Daddies have worried too much and look older than they should!

> O Lord, how happy we should be
> If we could cast our care on Thee,
> If we from self could rest,
> And feel at heart that One above,
> In perfect wisdom, perfect love,
> Is working for the best.

(f)God is as Good as His Word
(Psalm 91:7)

I want to tell you this morning a story about a wounded soldier. He was a soldier from the country of France. This young soldier was part of a great army which Napoleon, the great French general and emperor, led from France all the way to Russia, even to its capital city, Moscow. Then when the winter was coming on, all that great army turned about, retreated, defeated by the weather because the winter that year came on very, very suddenly and severely. I wonder if you could find out the year.

Have any of you boys and girls been to Seaton Park in August to hear the festival orchestra and see the fireworks? (You remember we have all these orchestras with young people from all over the world.) At a certain point in the open-air concert, this great orchestra plays a certain piece and with it we have these wonderful fireworks. It is a piece of music about a war - this war between France and Russia. It was written by the great Russian composer Tschaikovsky. It is called an overture - a piece often played at the beginning of an opera. This overture is called the 1812. That then was the year that all this happened. If your Mummies or Daddies have a record of this, ask them to let you hear it. There you will hear the war. You'll hear two national anthems: the French Marseillaise, which gets louder, and louder and then there is the clash of the armies, then you begin to hear the Russian national anthem and it begins to get on top. It ends with the bells of Moscow

pealing out that the Russians had defeated the
French and Napoleon was away back to France.

It was in 1812 then that our story happened.
Napoleon had set out from France with more than
half a million men. Then in the winter they had
turned back, and before the army reached France,
many of them were dead or had disappeared. But
this young French boy in the army had a godly
mother who gave him a promise (out of God's
Book) when he set out for the war. She said the
promise God had given to her was that he would
come back. He would not be killed, he would come
back. And this young French boy believed his
mother when she gave him this promise out of
God's Book, and although in that war he had many
near shaves he was still living and unwounded when
the army turned back to go home in the winter.

One day however, some Russian soldiers
surprised them. There was a fierce attack and the
boy was seriously wounded, and many of his com-
rades, French soldiers, lay around him dead. There
were Russian soldiers everywhere running back-
wards and forwards, and almost over him sometimes, so he thought it wise, although he was in great
pain to lie there as if he were dead in case any
Russian soldier came and wanted to finish him off.
So he lay there as if he was dead too and he prayed.
He prayed, he wondered and he feared. Then he
thought of his mother's promise out of God's
Word, that he would come back. The soldiers were
still rushing about there and so he kept his head
down and prayed and waited. Then it was quiet,
the soldiers had gone, moved on. He lifted his
head a little, and saw a soldier coming towards him,

so down went his head again. But he watched - kept his weather - eye open. When that soldier came towards him it wasn't a Russian soldier, but a soldier wearing a French uniform. The soldier came to him, looked at him, and picked him up - he was an older man and strong. He carried him for days, attending to his wounds as he ploughed through the snow till the boy was able to limp a little. So they came home and were safe.

He was safe because he believed the promise his mother gave him out of God's Word. She had prayed and believed God would protect her boy and bring him back to her. And God did, because, boys and girls, this is what God loves to do, to bring us back to Himself and save us because He loves us so.

> We have heard a joyful sound,
> > 'Jesus saves!'
> Spread the gladness all around;
> > 'Jesus saves!'
> Bear the news to every land,
> Climb the steeps and cross the waves;
> Onward tis our Lord's command.
> > 'Jesus saves!'

(g)God's Use of Evil
(Genesis50:20)

What do you know about Joseph? He was one of a family of thirteen children, twelve boys and one girl, Dinah. We are told he was his father's favourite and he gave him a very special present, a coat of many colours. It was very bad of his father Jacob to have such a favourite and it made his brothers very jealous. One day Joseph came with food to them when they were out in the country with their sheep and some of them said, "Here comes our father's favourite. Kill him, and we will say a wild beast has done it. We can dip his coat in blood from one of the animals and show it to our father." But Reuben, the eldest said, "No, he is our brother." So instead they put him in a pit - a hole in the ground, but later, when some travellers going to Egypt on their camels arrived, the brothers sold Joseph to them as a slave.

He became a slave in Egypt and although he was a good man there, he was put in prison. A wicked woman was angry with him and had him put in prison. There are people in prisons today, not because they have been bad, but because they are good and love Jesus. Isn't that awful? We were reading of some of them last night at the prayer meeting.

In prison, Joseph was able to do something for another prisoner who was there. He was the cup-bearer to the king, but he had done wrong. This man had a dream and Joseph was able to tell him what the dream meant. The cup-bearer got out of prison and resumed being cup-bearer to the king. He had to taste the king's wine to make sure it wasn't poisoned. At first he forgot about Joseph, then when Pharaoh (the king) had a dream and was disturbed by it he remembered and said, "There is a man in prison who interprets dreams (tells you what they mean)."

So Joseph was taken out. He listened to Pharaoh tell his dream and was able to interpret it: about the famine which was to come, how they should prepare for it, because it would last seven years and there would be very little food in the land. Pharaoh said, "That is very interesting. I would not have known my dream meant that. It is telling us to prepare for seven years of famine. We will need to gather all the grain we can, and put it into barns before the seven years of famine. That is wonderful. I think, Joseph, we will put you in charge of the country."

So he made Joseph, who was a foreigner, prime minister. But there came to be famine not only in Egypt but in Jacob's country. He said, "What can we do? We hear there is food in Egypt. They have it in barns there." So Jacob sent his sons down to Egypt. They came to Joseph but they did not know it was Joseph, he was so different from what he had been years ago. Joseph knew them, but they did not know him. He kept them for a time, and then at last (to cut a long story short) he said, "I am Joseph, your brother." I suppose they thought he was dead, or a slave somewhere, but he was in charge of the whole country. What a shock they got. They were frightened. What would happen to them? So they said they were sorry. They had better, hadn't they? Then Joseph said this, "You meant it for bad, when

you sold me as a slave, or would have killed me; but
God meant it for good." Even old Jacob himself
went to Egypt because there was food there.

I can think of another Man who was badly
treated and yet God blessed Him. He could have
said, "You meant it for evil, but God meant it for
good." Who is that other Man? There is a sign of
that other Man in church somewhere, if you can see
it. Who is that other Man that was treated so badly?

"Jesus."

Where is the sign, then? Yes, the cross over the
pulpit. They treated Jesus badly and shed His blood.
But Jesus said, "You Jews and you Romans meant
it for bad. You wanted to destroy the best Man who
ever lived. But God meant it for good, that you
might be saved through My precious blood."

Thy everlasting truth,
Father, Thy ceaseless love,
Sees all thy children's wants, and knows
What best for each will prove.

(h)Satan
(1Peter 5:8-11)

I am going to speak to you about the devil. Who made the devil? God made the devil. But He did not make him bad, did He? God couldn't make anything bad. We read at the beginning of the Bible that God made everything good: the world, the sun, the moon, the stars, the trees, the rivers, the animals, the birds, and our first parents, Adam and Eve. He made everything perfectly good.

How is it that if God made the devil he is so bad? Well, the devil was made one of the brightest angels. I think he was the very brightest angel of all. He was so wonderful and so beautiful that he became very proud. He said, "God has made me so beautiful that I think I could go and sit on His throne." That is what he wanted to do. But God could not allow someone that He had made, any creature that He had made, to take His throne; that is impossible. What did God do? He said, "Down, down, DOWN!" He cast him down. But the devil was so mad that he said, "I will do all I can to hurt You, God, for doing this to me. I will hurt all that You have made and especially I will hurt men and women, and boys and girls." He was mad.

He thought up two different ways to try to hurt God: two opposite ways. One way was to come before men and women, boys and girls like an angel of light. He had been a bright angel and is still a spirit, so he comes before people and says, "Look, I am from God and I am holy, and good, and true; follow me." But it is a lie. He is trying to take people away from God and from the Lord Jesus

Christ. That is one way that he tries to hurt God and God's people, to charm them. Then he will destroy them. The other way is to frighten them. That is what we were reading this morning (1 Peter 5:8-11) about the devil like a roaring lion chasing after people to devour them, to eat them up.

So we have to watch the devil in two ways. One way he tries is to charm us and lead us astray trying to show how nice he is. That is how he tempted Eve: "Oh, eat the fruit of that tree. God said you shouldn't but it is really very nice - eat it." And Adam and Eve fell and became sinful. The other way is to chase and chase us to terrify us. We have to watch that too. We have to watch and say, "Here is the roaring lion. What are we going to do?" Run to Jesus. Jesus has got the victory over the devil. Although God made the devil and he went astray, Jesus died on the cross and defeated the devil. What we have to do when Satan comes and charms us on the one hand and frightens us on the other, is to run to Jesus and say, "Oh, don't let that deceiver lead me astray." Run to Jesus and He will protect you. He will watch over you. That is what we are to sing about now.

> There's a wicked spirit
>   Watching round you still
> And he tries to tempt you
> To all harm and ill.
>
> But ye must not hear him
> Though 'tis hard for you
> To resist the evil,
>   And the good to do.

Section Nine

Teaching Children On Special Occasions

The so-called festivals of the Christian year have become fraught with so many worldly associations and even commemorations become so changed that their original meaning is lost. It is important for children that the centralities of our faith and history are not forgotten or turned into something else.

(a) Easter
(Philippians 3:20,21)

Do you know the word "seasons"? If we lived in certain countries that are very, very hot we would not know the seasons so well because they do not change as much as ours do. We have Spring, Summer, Autumn, Winter. When it grows dark early in the day, that is winter, then the cold comes and the snow. Then comes the Spring and the days get longer, then on to Summer and then on to Autumn and then Winter again.

Nature seems to go to sleep during the winter. You do not see so many birds, and the leaves fall off the trees and there are not so many flowers. But when Spring comes, everything comes to life. The birds begin to flutter and make their nests. I was watching a little blue-tit in a little bird house next door to me this morning. It went out and in, making its nest; it was wonderful to see. The eggs will be laid, and they will burst, and the little birds come out. The flowers will bloom and then we will be into summer. In the autumn the flowers die and we see less and less of the birds, and then it is winter with long, long, dark nights. Then lighter and warmer. So it happens each year. The flowers fade and the plants die, but up they come again next year.

All that speaks of Jesus' resurrection. Just as the bird breaks the shell of the egg with its beak and out comes the chicken or nestling in the Springtime, so Jesus was raised from the dead out of the tomb. But Jesus was raised from the dead in Springtime, at Easter, only once; the flowers come up every year. When Jesus was raised from the dead

He was given a new body. It was the same and yet it was not the same; it was different from the body He had before He died. He really died. His heart stopped beating and His breath went and He was laid in the tomb. All Friday night, all day Saturday, into Sunday morning He lay in the tomb, and then, before it was light, God came and said, "Jesus, get up!" He got up but His body was changed. It was so changed that it would never, never die. Jesus is up in heaven now. He is up there with His new body and it is as bright and new and shining today as it was nearly two thousand years ago when He was raised from the dead. And it will last forever.

All who believe in the Lord Jesus are going to be given the same kind of body as He now has. One day, if you love Jesus and follow Him, you are going to have a body like His that will never grow old. It will never wear out. It will never get sick and it will never die. That is what we are thinking about today: because Jesus is the first man to have a body which will not wear out, all those who love Jesus (and those who loved Him and have gone to heaven) are all going to have new bodies that are never going to wear out or die. Isn't that wonderful? We are very happy. People who love the Lord Jesus are looking forward to the time when they will have bodies that will never be sore, never have pain, never be sick and will never be tired. It is wonderful; they will never die again. Wonderful!

(b) Whitsun
(Acts 2)

Today is Whitsun. Those of you who are at school and learning to read and write letters how would you spell 'Whitsunday'? W-H-I-T-S-U-N-D-A-Y. But the old way of writing that was Whitesunday - WHITE SUNDAY.

Why Whitesunday? Well, on Whitesunday in days of old, lots of people used to come to be baptised and they wore white dresses for this. So, it was called Whitesunday. But Whitsun means something more than white dresses. It was the day on which God sent the Holy Spirit from heaven. Jesus had gone back there after His resurrection. On that day of Pentecost, fifty days after Jesus had been raised from the dead, He sent the Spirit to the disciples, just as God had sent the Spirit to rest on Him.

Now, *when* did God send His Spirit on Jesus? Do you remember when God sent His Spirit upon Jesus? What was happening to Jesus when the Spirit came? Was He in Jerusalem? Was He in the mountains, or was it by the river? Do you not remember? It was when He was being baptised in the river Jordan by John the Baptist. He went down into the Jordan to be baptised and as He came up from the water, something happened. What happened? People saw something, it wasn't a kite, nor a shining light - but a dove.

Why did God send a dove on the head of Jesus when He was baptised? What is special about a dove? Is a dove like an eagle or a hawk? No, it is the opposite. It is gentle. A dove speaks of peace. I have seen doves fighting, but not often, because they are gentle birds. When God sent the dove to light on Jesus' head at His baptism, God was very pleased. He said, "This is My beloved Son in whom I am well pleased." He was pleased with His Son because He went through baptism for us. When Jesus, up in heaven, sent His Spirit down upon the disciples that were gathered in the upper room - one hundred and twenty of them - something also lighted on their heads. But it wasn't a dove; it was tongues of fire.

Why is it that God sent a dove on Jesus' head, and tongues of fire on the disciples' heads? Do you know why that would have been? God needs to show a difference between the Spirit coming on Jesus and on the disciples; the difference between peace and tongues of fire. There was no sin in Jesus throughout His life. He never sinned one sin. We, poor things, are sinning all the time, naughty creatures that we are, aren't we? So when God sent His Spirit down upon the disciples He was saying, "Oh, you are Mine but you are dirty. You need to be cleaned, not only by the precious blood of Jesus to wash away your sins, but you need your sins to be burned out by the holy fire of My Spirit."

Now, never forget that. We need to be cleansed, not only by Jesus' blood, but by His Holy Spirit purging us from our sins.

(c)Communion and Harvest
(Genesis 1:11-12)

This is our Autumn Communion and it is also the time of Harvest Thanksgiving, when we thank God for providing all that we need - food for our bodies especially, and food for our souls.

We have seeds here and fruits, then on the Communion Table we have bread. Seeds of course come from plants. I have some here: a plum seed. That's the big, hard one. These dark ones are apple seeds. These are oats. If we had wheat the seeds would give us flour for bread like the bread on the table.

Let us think about seeds. Jesus said concerning seeds that unless you plant them in the ground, making them die, then nothing will come of them, they would just remain seeds. But when you plant seed like corn in the ground, the outside dies and rots away because of the dampness of the soil. But inside there is the germ hidden in the seed, seeming so dead, until you put it in the ground, when it comes to life. There is not only the germ but food for the germ to grow with. So, it grows, and grows, and grows till we have flowers or corn, and so on.

Seeds come f rom plants, as we have been reading in Genesis chapters one and two. The plants came first and then the seeds; the chicken first and then the egg, is what the Bible says. From the plants we have the flowers, the buds, the fruit and the seeds, and we plant them in the ground.

I want you to think of our Jesus as a beautiful plant. The Bible speaks of Him as the Rose of Sharon and the Lily of the Valleys - beautiful, sweet-smelling, fragrant plants. I want you to think of Jesus as a beautiful plant and then of the seed from that beautiful plant, Jesus' life and death, which He takes and plants in our breasts. He plants His own seed, the seed that comes from His dying and rising from the dead, in our hearts. When He plants His seed there, that puts to death the bad part of us, the naughty part, the sinful part, the part that God does not like.

You remember that Satan sowed seed in man's heart. From what we were reading in the early chapters of Genesis, you remember it was Satan who sowed his evil seed in the heart of Adam and Eve. But when Jesus plants His seed in our hearts, through His death and rising from the dead, that puts to death the bad part. The good part, the Jesus part, begins to grow.

It grows and grows and grows until you look at a little boy or a little girl, especially when they are loving and kind, and saying "Yes" to Mummy and not "No", being brave when they are hurt or sick, sharing something with their friends at school or at play, and you say, "Ah, I think I can see the beginnings of Jesus in that little boy or that little girl, because the seed that Jesus planted in their breasts has begun to grow."

He can plant the seed when you are very, very young. He puts to death the bad, and the good grows, and grows, and grows until we begin to see Jesus in little boys and girls, and in bigger boys and bigger girls, and in men and women. We are here this morning to be helped to grow more and more like Jesus. I hope we will. I think we will.

Hymn: We plough the fields and scatter.........

(d)Rememberance
(2 Corinthians 9)

Boys and girls, you see I am holding some poppies in my hand and most people here are wearing poppies. Now, why is it, do you think that we wear poppies today? Yes, we are remembering people who died in the war and remembering too of course,(which is why we come to Church on Sunday), someone special who died - Jesus.

Why do we wear a red flower? We could wear other coloured flowers: white, yellow, or blue. Why do you think it should be red? That's right - it stands for peoples' blood. Between seventy and eighty years ago these people whose names are written there on the war memorial died, some of them on Flanders field where Flanders poppies grow. On these battle fields up grew these lovely Flanders poppies to speak of the blood which was shed to give us our liberty.

Look at the names on this part of our War Memorial. These men, who once sat in Church like you spilt their blood on the battle fields in the First World War so that we would not become slaves to other people. Then on the other part of the Memorial are the names of those who died in the Second World War. They also gave their lives so that we could go free. Look higher to that red cross on the pulpit light. That speaks of One who gave His life that we should be free in heaven with Him forever. We are going to sing about Him and as we sing about Him we will think of them.

(e)Christmas

Now, you know that Jesus was not born in an ordinary house like yours or mine; he was born in a stable where animals live, because there was no room for him in the inn (the hotel). He was born in the kind of place you might call an outhouse, or stable. Have you ever been in a byre, or stable for horses? It usually has a cobbled stone floor, straw to lie on - quite warm - and hay to eat. And because there is so much straw, hay and especially corn there, there are often lots of mice running about. Sometimes whole families of mice make their home in a barn and live there quite happily. They may even make friends with the other animals.

I am going to tell you about a family of mice, who lived in the stable where Jesus was born, in a great crack in the wall near the floor. There they fed and became fat mice living on the corn that was given to the oxen and the donkeys. On the night on which Jesus was born, Father Mouse, called Nathan, but he had the nickname of "Fleet-foot" because he could run very fast, had been out paying a visit to some of his relations down the road. On the way back he saw that a man and a woman with a donkey had arrived and were making themselves at home. So he darted round the side of the stable until he was opposite the crack and slipped quietly home without anyone seeing him. And as soon as he got home he told Mrs. Mouse whose name was Martha because she was a very busy little lady mouse, and the children - there were seven of them, all with Jewish mouse names. He told them all about the man and the woman.

You will have guessed, won't you, that it was Mary and Joseph who had come to stay the night in their stable. He warned them all that they must not go out without taking special care, because the more animals and people in the stable, the more danger there was of little mice getting caught and even killed.

But Father Mouse himself was a very inquisitive fellow and he could not keep his little nose away from the opening of that crack to see what was happening. He sat and watched, and listened. He saw that Joseph was very busy attending to Mary, and then, what do you think? Yes, Nathan heard the cry of a human baby. He could hardly believe his ears. After quite a long time he said to himself, "I must go out and see what is happening in that stable. I want to see that baby."

So out he went, as carefully as he could. But Joseph was so busy attending to Mary and to a little bundle that was lying in the donkey's feeding plate (the manger), that Nathan was able to come right out and climb up the side of the wall to get a better view of everything. There was Mary. Joseph had made a lovely bed for her in the straw, and there was the baby lying in its manger bed. It looked such a lovely child that Nathan, Fleet-foot, said, "I think that is the most beautiful human child I have ever seen. I must take a closer look." So he climbed down the wall as quietly as he could, which was very quiet indeed, and across the floor and actually climbed the side of the wooden manger until he was almost at the top. And what do you think? Yes, he was looking down on the Christ child, the baby Jesus, lying sound asleep. Father Mouse thought he had never seen such a pretty face in all his life, so he crouched there a long time, just looking, looking, looking until there was a sound from Joseph and he thought he had better get out of the way.

When he got home, he said to his family, mother Martha, Simon, Andrew, Bartholomew, Matthias, Hannah, Sarah and Elizabeth: four boys and three girl mice. "Oh, I have seen the most beautiful sight: a baby child with the face of an angel - a new-born baby human. O Mummy Martha, you must see it. I don't know how but you must see this child's face."

So Daddy Mouse took up his place at the opening of the crack, which was their home and he watched, and waited, and listened. Soon everything became perfectly quiet, there was hardly a sound except for Joseph's loud breathing. He was asleep and so was Mary and the babe. Nathan said to Mummy Martha, "My dear, *now* is the time. Come quickly and be ever so quiet."

"Don't you tell me," said Mother Mouse. "Do you think I'd do anything silly when I might get caught? What would those darling little mice do, and what would you do Nathan if I got caught and killed?"

Out she slipped so quickly and smoothly on her little feet that you would think she was on skis. Father Mouse had told her exactly where to go, and soon she was on top of the manger looking down at the loveliest baby face she had ever seen. "Yes," said Martha. "It is the sweetest face I have ever seen," and she sat crouched there on top of the manger watching until she almost forgot where she was and had to remind herself that if anyone stirred she was in great danger. But already Fleet-foot had come out to see where his wife had got to and led her safely home again.

Back home she told the baby mice all about seeing the most beautiful face in the world. "What's such a beautiful child doing in a stable?" asked Nathan.

"I do not know," said Martha. "But that's a very special child, I reckon, and whatever he is doing here, I think we are greatly honoured to have had such a child born in our humble stable. You know," she went on, "Daddy Mouse, we don't know how long that beautiful child may be here. It may be gone by morning. I would like the children to see it. What do you think, Daddy?"

"Well," said Father Mouse, "that's an awful risk to take, Mummy; you know how clumsy and silly these youngsters are. How could seven of them go and stand on top of the manger and look in? One is sure to nudge the other and one will fall in and wake the child, or even harm him, which would be terrible. And our whole lives would be in danger. Or they might giggle and misbehave, wakening the man and woman."

"Oh no," said Mother Mouse. "I won't let you speak about my darling children in that way. They are very sensible when there is danger. After all, none of them has ever got caught, although I must admit that little Simon has been very near it, more than once. If Simon behaves, the others will."

So it was agreed that one at a time the baby mice would climb up and have a look at the baby's lovely face. Martha was to stand by the door of the crack, Nathan at the foot of the manger, and so they would guide each little mouse - the eldest first, and right on to the youngest until every one had had a chance to see the beautiful baby's face, like the face of an angel. They behaved perfectly. Well, they were afraid first of all, and then when they saw that face, they all became very, very good. Only, they wanted to stay longer and just look. It seemed as if the baby's face did something to the little mice so that they crouched as if they were in a kind of dream or trance as big people would call it - and they could hardly come away - even Simon. He thought it a huge joke at first, although he had promised to be good, but when he got to the top of the manger and looked in, he caught his breath. When he got back, he said to his Mummy, "I never saw anything so beautiful in all my life."

Morning came and the stable door opened. Out went Joseph. He had gone for some water, and while he was away, in flew a gorgeous bird. It was the kind of bird I saw when I was in Bethlehem a few years ago. It was soft light brown, with lovely soft blue wings. It was such a pretty bird, bigger than a sparrow and even bigger than a thrush or blackbird - a bit like a cuckoo, I would say. I looked in all the bookshops in Jerusalem, where Jesus was crucified, and in all the bigger shops in Tel Aviv, which is a very grand city indeed, but I could not find in the whole of the Holy Land a book about the birds which lived there. Anyway, this lovely bird flew into the stable. What was it doing there?

Mummy Mouse was at the entrance to their crack-home when the bird flew in and saw it perch there on the rafters and sit looking down on the manger with the lovely child in it. The bird watched for a long time and then quietly fluttered to another rafter to be nearer. There it was, looking down on the baby, the holy child. He sat there a long time just watching. Then Mother Mouse made a slight movement. He saw her and said in bird language, "What are you doing here? Better watch what you do, that's a special child, you know."

"I'm sure he is," said Martha. "But beautiful bird, this is our home. We live here, and this man and this woman came here last night. Their beautiful baby was born shortly afterwards and we've all been up to the top of the manger to look at him. Isn't he a lovely child? I've never seen such a lovely baby, have you, Mr. Bird?"

"So, you have been up there have you? How dare you, little mouse. Do you not know what child that is? How dare you go and look at him."

"Oh!" cried Martha, "I hope we haven't done anything wrong, Mr. Bird. (We will call him Mr. Softy because the colours of his brown and blue feathers were so soft.) We did not mean to do wrong," she whispered, "but Nathan said he was so lovely we had all to see him before they took him away. We might never see such a beautiful baby again."

"Well, you never shall," said Mr. Softy, rather sternly. "For that is a unique child, that is," he said grunting as if he was very proud of himself for using such a word.

"But what is 'unique'?" asked Mrs. Mouse. "I don't understand these difficult words."

"It means," said Softy, sticking out his chest as if he was a professor, "that there will never be another child like him. He is the only one. He is not an ordinary child at all, you see. That child is God's Son."

"God's Son," said Mrs. Mouse. "You don't say! How could God's Son be born in a stable?"

"Well, he is," said Mr. Softy, looking a bit soft but rather clever. "He is God's eternal Son, that's who he is."

"There you go again," said Martha. "You use such dreadfully difficult words. What's eternal?"

"Eternal," said Professor Softy, looking even more wise, "means that he will live forever. He never had a beginning and he will never have an end. He'll never die. Well, he will die, but he will rise again from the dead and then he will live forever, if you get my meaning," he said a little more kindly and humbly.

"But, who told you all this?" asked Mrs. Mouse, suddenly wondering why she was listening to all this strange talk from a bird. What did birds know that little mice didn't?

"I'll tell you," said Mr. - sorry - Professor Bird. (We'll not call him Mr. Softy anymore; he is too wise for a name like that, however soft his colours are.) "I was sleeping in my tree, out on the shepherds' fields, not many hundreds of yards from here, as birds fly, when I heard a commotion, some kind of noise, and the shepherds, who often sleep under my tree, - (though there are always one or two watching for wild beasts who might steal and kill their sheep) - were sitting up, looking towards the sky. When I looked up I saw that the sky was full of light - a great patch of light in the darkness and there was an angel ready to speak."

"What did he say?" asked Martha.

"He said, 'Don't be afraid, you shepherds down there, for I have come to bring you good news and you must tell it to everyone else. There is born for you this day, in the town of Bethlehem, a Saviour, who is Christ the Lord. You will find him in a stable, lying in a manger.' Then the whole sky was bright with crowds of angels all saying together, 'Glory to God in the highest, and on earth peace to those whom God delights to favour.' Then the light disappeared. That was all. So that, Mrs. Mouse, is how I know that he is a special child."

Good Christian men, rejoice
With heart and soul and voice!
Give ye heed to what we say:
News! News!
Jesus Christ is born today.
Ox and ass before Him bow,
And He is in the manger now:
Christ is born today.

Christian Focus Publications Ltd.
are to shortly publish more books
by William Still.

They will include

(1) His Autobiography

(2) Another volume of Children's
Addresses